PROFESSIONAL SELF-HELP GUIDES

Living with

Each book in this series will deal with a chronic, serious disease or condition. It will contain background and medical information on causes and symptoms and will explain treatment in some detail – both practical (drug treatments, surgery) and psychological (self-help, home care, social implications)

published with this title

Living with breast cancer and mastectomy
NICHOLAS TARRIER

Living with

stress and anxiety

A self-help guide

BOB WHITMORE

 Manchester University Press

COPYRIGHT © BOB WHITMORE 1987

Published by MANCHESTER UNIVERSITY PRESS
Oxford Road, Manchester M13 9PL, UK
and 27 South Main Street, Wolfeboro, NH 03894-2069, USA

British Library cataloguing in publication data
Whitmore, R.J.
Living with stress and anxiety.
1. Anxiety
I. Title
616.85'223   RC531

Library of Congress cataloging in publication data applied for

ISBN 0-7190-1887-0 *hardback*
ISBN 0-7190-1952-4 *paperback*

Typeset by Hems & Co, Turners Lane, Gillingham, Dorset
Printed in Great Britain
by Bell & Bain Limited, Glasgow

Contents

Preface   *page* vii
Acknowledgements   viii

Introduction   1

PART ONE   What is anxiety?   5
1   The three sides of anxiety   6
2   The physical side of anxiety: the stress response   10
3   The psychological side of anxiety   18
4   The behavioural side of anxiety   30
5   Anxiety: why me? Stressful life events and life strains   36
6   The three sides of anxiety, life events and life strains:
        how they relate together   48

PART TWO   Coping with stress and anxiety   53
7   Relaxation training and physical exercise   56
8   Psychological methods   64
9   Behavioural targets   72
10 Coping with stressful life events and life strains   78
11 Putting it all together in a self-help programme   83
12 Tranquillisers and anxiety   89
13 Summary   91

APPENDIX I   Progressive relaxation training   94
APPENDIX II   Suggestions for further reading   100

Preface

Anxiety is perhaps the most common psychological problem in industrial societies today. People exhibiting the various signs of anxiety represent a large proportion of the average GP's caseload. A great deal of research has been undertaken in recent years which has helped us to understand anxiety and, hence, help people overcome its serious negative consequences; it is one of the aims of this book to inform a wider readership of the results of this recent research.

Although there is still a great deal to discover, we are closer now to understanding the nature and causes of anxiety, and successful therapeutic approaches have been developed to overcoming its most damaging effects. The majority of people who experience anxiety remain unaware of these advances, and, unfortunately, this is true of some professionals (GPs, social workers, nurses, workers in voluntary organisations and so on) who come across sufferers of anxiety and stress in the course of their work. This book has been written to help both these groups of people.

Part One consists of chapters dealing with the various signs or symptoms of anxiety; what causes them, what they mean, how they affect people. Each chapter includes a probe questionnaire which the sufferer answers in order to build up a picture of his or her particular anxiety problem. Part Two builds on the knowledge the reader has acquired in Part One by describing those therapeutic techniques which have been found to be most effective in dealing with anxiety and stress. Using the answers to the probe questionnaires from Part One the reader is shown how to use these techniques to construct his or her own detailed self-help programme.

Acknowledgements

I would firstly like to acknowledge Alan Tatham and Vicki Coletta, with whom I wrote a self-help booklet on anxiety, portions of which were used as a basis for several sections in this book. My thanks also to Claire Holditch for her useful comments on an earlier draft of the book. Wendy Spencer had to live with the stress of translating my manuscript before typing it out, and I would like to thank her for her patience and helpfulness. Finally, my thanks to all those people who have experienced anxiety with whom I have had contact, and who both directly and indirectly have helped in formulating this book, which I therefore dedicate to them.

Introduction

WHO THIS BOOK IS FOR

As we shall see later in this book, stress and anxiety are normal parts of human life; we all experience different degrees of tension each day, often even without knowing that we are tense. For some people though, the tension or anxiety they feel is so high that it seriously interferes with their lives. Anxiety can affect people in many different ways, and the following are very brief descriptions of the three general sorts of difficulties people may experience.

PHOBIC ANXIETY

A phobia is a very powerful, specific fear of certain things (animals or situations) which is completely out of proportion to the real threat involved. Most people would feel nervous standing on the edge of a cliff but, for example, a woman who is phobic of heights will not only avoid standing on cliff edges, but will also avoid situations (bridges, tall buildings) where the danger of falling is tiny or non-existent. Similarly many people dislike insects but a person who is, for example, phobic of wasps may avoid going out in the warm summer months just in case he or she is stung by one.

GENERAL SITUATIONAL ANXIETY

More common than phobic anxiety, this sort of anxiety is not as specific as a phobia, the anxiety occurring in a range of **related** situations. To take an example, a man may experience anxiety in **social** situations: in pubs, at work and so on. We cannot say that he is 'person phobic' as there are quite a few situations involving people when he does not feel anxious, such as when he is out with his wife. However, in places where there are a lot of people he feels panicky and so avoids these places as much as possible, seriously interfering with his life.

NON-SPECIFIC TENSION

This sort of anxiety, which is very common, is basically a continuous high level of tension. The person who experiences this may never feel panicky in specific situations, but will rather feel continuously 'on edge'. He or she will find it very hard to relax, will be always worrying about things, and will over-react to problems. When it is mild, this sort of anxiety may not seriously disrupt the person's life, in that he or she does not avoid situations (unlike the other two sorts of anxiety). However, even when it is mild it does seriously reduce the **quality** of life, and when the anxiety level is very high, the person who experiences it may find day-to-day life very hard.

With any kind of anxiety difficulty, there may also be 'secondary' problems, such as tension headaches, insomnia, general aches and pains, irritability. These are a few examples of the sorts of problems of which people who experience main complaint—but as we will see later in this book these problems can often be most usefully seen as part of a more general anxiety or stress difficulty.

Although these three sorts of anxiety have been described in very general terms, most people who feel they have anxiety difficulties will probably be able to see their problem as being in one of the three areas, and it is for these people that this book will be useful, as well as for those who are interested in the subject of stress and anxiety. However, it is not really necessary to 'label' anxiety in this way, it is more important to (i) understand what anxiety is and (ii) work out a plan to deal with it.

The next section suggests how best to use the book to achieve these goals.

HOW TO USE THIS BOOK

Living with stress and anxiety is split into two parts. The first part sets out to explain what anxiety is, in some detail, for this reason: virtually everyone who has experienced anxiety, particularly severe anxiety, has had that anxiety intensified by lack of understanding of what was happening to him or her. **Understanding** anxiety is, therefore, the first step in learning to deal with it, and that is why the first half of this book is devoted to explaining the various signs or symptoms of anxiety and how they all relate together. At the end of each chapter there is a brief questionnaire looking at those points discussed in the chapter which apply to the reader in particular. It is important that these questions are answered because the information in the questionnaire will be brought together and used later in the book.

Part Two describes the three related ways of dealing with those anxiety signs which are looked at in detail in Part One. The goal of Part Two is for the reader to write his or her own self-help plan to help him or her to overcome or minimise anxiety. The emphasis is on the various **skills** the reader can learn and how these skills can be put to use in real life. As we shall see, for many people this will involve confronting situations which are, for them, fear-inducing, so the approach outlined in this book is essentially practical and is based as far as possible on well researched techniques and theories, as well as the clinical experience of the author. Reading this book by itself will probably not solve an anxiety problem, the reader will also need to learn and **apply** the information and the various skills described here.

Part one

What is anxiety?

1 The three sides of anxiety

Many words are used to describe the experiences people have and what they do when they are anxious, such as nerves, phobias, stress, fear, panic, and so on. For the sake of simplicity in this book we will use the words **anxiety** and **tension** to cover all of them.

Each of these three words gives a general idea of what people experience but we need to be more specific about that experience if we are to understand it. In fact, if we look at the experience of anxiety in detail we can see that it can be split into three categories:

1 The physical signs of anxiety
2 The psychological signs of anxiety
3 The behavioural signs of anxiety

(Throughout this book we use the word 'sign' instead of the often used 'symptom'. This is because the approach of this book sees anxiety as part of **normal** human behaviour and experience (if exaggerated). 'Symptom', however, implies underlying **illness** which does not fit in with this approach.)

To illustrate these three sides of anxiety in more detail, let us look at a situation in which a high level of anxiety would occur in **anybody**:

Elaine Briggs is about to undergo her first parachute jump. She is doing it for charity on a weekend training course and is now waiting in a group at the airfield for her turn to go up in a light aeroplane to make the jump. Elaine feels very frightened. She is aware of her heart racing and a tight feeling in her chest and stomach. She is breathing very quickly. She and other members of the group all feel the need to go to the toilet, even though most have already been several times that morning. In her mind she keeps going over all the safety rules she has been taught in case her main parachute fails. She also imagines what would happen if her main parachute failed to open and she panicked instead of opening the reserve parachute. She imagines the terror of plunging towards the ground. She feels even more anxious when she imagines that, and she considers avoiding the jump. She imagines going up to the trainer and telling him that she feels too ill to do it. The thought is tempting and she thinks about how relieved she would feel knowing that she did not have to jump. However, she also thinks about what everyone else would say, especially those who sponsored her, and she decides to face the jump instead.

When she climbs into the small aeroplane her heart is pounding very hard and her breathing feels tight and restricted. She feels more frightened than ever before but makes herself think about what she has to do, and when the trainer sitting alongisde her tells her, she steps out onto the wheel of the plane, hanging on to the wing strut just as she was taught. When he shouts, 'Go', off she leaps. Before she knows it the parachute has opened and she is floating down. She feels utterly relieved and very happy when a few minutes later she lands safely. She also feels very proud that she did not avoid the jump.

Let us now look at all the various signs of anxiety the parachutist experienced in terms of the three sides of anxiety:

The physical signs of anxiety
1 Her heart pounded
2 She felt the urge to go to the toilet
3 Her chest and stomach muscles felt very tight
4 She was breathing very quickly

The psychological signs of anxiety
5 She felt frightened and nervous
6 She pictured in her mind's eye what would happen if her 'chute failed to open and she panicked and imagined falling
7 She imagined avoiding doing the jump and how relieved she would feel if she didn't have to do it
8 She also imagined how guilty she would feel if she did avoid it

The behavioural signs of anxiety
9 She went to the toilet several times before the jump

We can see that the various experiences Elaine had and what she did fit into one of these three sides of anxiety: the physical, the psychological and the behavioural. If we want to give a full description of a person's anxiety, we must look at it from each of these different angles. This, in fact, is what psychologists and physiologists interested in anxiety research have found, whether they are studying anxiety in parachutists, business executives, people suffering from phobias (for example, an extreme fear of dogs) and so on.

Of course every person's experience of anxiety is different in that one of the three sides of anxiety is often stronger than the other two. If we look at our parachutist again, we can see that she had four physical signs and four psychological signs, but she only had one behavioural sign, that of going to the toilet, and this was not significant.

Let us imagine that Elaine followed through one of the psychological signs, and she decided to tell the trainer that she feels too ill to do the jump and so does not do it. Added on to the list of behavioural signs would be this:

10 She told the trainer she felt too ill and so **avoided** the jump

This, then, becomes the most significant of all the signs. In Chapter 4 we will see how avoidance is often the most important part of anxiety, the one that interferes with people's lives and most. For our parachutist, avoiding the jump will not be serious as she won't need to it in in the future. However, if a person avoids going into social situations, for example work, because of anxiety, we can see that his or her anxiety problem involving behavioural avoidance is more serious. In the following chapter we will look at each of the three sides in more detail.

SUMMARY

The experience of anxiety (nerves, fear, etc.) is best understood by looking at it as having three different sides. These are:

1 **The physical side:** palpitations, butterflies and so on
2 **The psychological side:** feeling frightened and thinking about what might happen very negatively
3 **The behavioural side:** avoiding doing things because of fear.

Every person with anxiety difficulties will probably experience the signs of one of the three parts more than the other, for example a person may be especially disturbed by physical signs. Also some signs are likely to be more serious in terms of interfering with people's lives. Those which lead to **avoiding** situations are likely to be particularly disruptive in this way.

PROBE QUESTIONNAIRE

Please spend some time completing this questionnaire. If you are not sure about anything just go back and check over the previous chapter. Think about the last time you felt particularly anxious.

On a piece of paper, write down under each of the following headings which signs you experienced.

1 **Physical signs** (those bodily sensations you had)

2 **Psychological signs** (what emotions you felt and the specific thoughts you had)

3 **Behavioural signs** (what you actually did)

2 The physical side of anxiety: the stress response

The physical side of anxiety is perhaps the most noticeable and disturbing part of anxiety which people experience, so to begin we will just list many of the physical signs of which people complain. This list is not exhaustive and some of the signs can be caused by things other than anxiety, but generally speaking when people complain of anxiety they will experience at least some of the following signs:

1 Heart racing (palpitations)
2 Stomach churning, butterflies in the stomach
3 Needing to go to the toilet, diarrhoea
4 Muscle tension in any part of the body, particularly stomach, neck, head
5 Tension headaches
6 Legs feeling 'like jelly'
7 Feeling sick
8 'Cold' sweat
9 Feeling dizzy
10 Breathing very quickly
11 Dry mouth
12 Difficulty swallowing
13 Tingling sensations, pins and needles
14 Feeling 'shaky'
15 Feeling flushed

As we have already said, people will probably not be aware of experiencing all of those signs, and of those they do experience some will feel worse than others. For example, a man may be particularly concerned about palpitations and for him this sign is the most distressing. Another person may find dizziness the main problem. Whatever, the important thing to understand is that whichever physical sign is most distressing, it will be part of a larger range of bodily sensations, which we will call the **stress response**.

The stress response is a mechanism which we all have and which is responsible for all the signs outlined above. The purpose of the stress response is essentially to prepare us for danger by increasing the general arousal of our bodies so we can deal with the danger more efficiently than when we are in our usual 'relaxed' state. Before describing the stress response in more detail, let us look at two examples of when it might be activated:

(a) A man is walking down a street when he sees a friend on the opposite side of the road. Without looking and because there isn't much traffic about he steps out to cross the road. He immediately hears a car horn and a screech of brakes. Without thinking he immediately leaps back on to the pavement and is left feeling shaky, with his heart racing and breathing heavily.

(b) A woman is walking down a quiet, poorly lit street at night, not far from her house. Suddenly she hears someone behind her, running towards her. She immediately feels very frightened, her heart races and she feels the compulsion to run for home, which is what she does, running faster than she thought she could and getting home safe and sound. She is left feeling very shaky and nervous.

For both these people, what has happened is that a split-second after they perceived danger their stress response was 'switched on'.

The stress response is quite complex, but briefly it prepares you for danger by causing the following things to happen to your body within a very short period of time (less than a second):

1 Your heart rate shoots up. It does this so that an increased amount of blood (energy) is pumped to various muscles, those of the arms and legs in particular as it is your arms and legs which are most likely to get you out of danger. Blood pressure, therefore, also increases.

2 In order to keep the heart beating (pumping) at this higher rate, your breathing rate increases to give the heart the extra energy (oxygen) it needs.

3 Because of the increased blood supply going to the various muscles, they become more tense, more ready to spring into action. The legs often feel 'shaky'

because of this. (Interestingly, although they may feel shaky and 'like jelly' they are in fact stronger than usual.)

4 Because your arms and legs need extra blood for the muscles, much of the blood which usually goes to service the stomach area is redirected away from the stomach (which can cope with a reduced blood supply during this emergency) and is sent instead to the arms and legs. This causes the 'churning' feeling in the stomach, 'butterflies', as well as diarrhoea, as digestion is temporarily affected.

5 As extra energy is being 'burned up' your temperature increases, so you perspire more to cool your body down. In extreme states of fear small blood vessels at the surface of the body, including the face, receive a reduced blood supply as well, so you go pale. (Some researchers believe that this is so that if you are physically damaged the reduced blood supply to the surface ensures less blood loss.) At less extreme states, however, you may feel flushed.

6 As your breathing rate increases, along with your heart rate, this affects the blood supply to the brain and so you feel light-headed or dizzy.

This is a brief simplified description of the stress response. The most important way the stress response causes these changes (such as increased heart rate) is by the release of chemicals into the blood supply which increase the activity of the heart and other organs. Perhaps the most well known of these chemicals is the hormone adrenaline. People can be made artificially anxious by injecting them with adrenaline. (Adrenaline also affects the emotions so that you feel 'worked up' and anxious.) However, for our purpose here, there are three things that should be noted:

1 The stress response is **automatic**. It is switched on without any conscious decisions being made. In the first example, (a), in particular, we can see that if the man had had to consciously decide the extent of the danger, he would have been run over before he had even noticed that it was a car that was coming towards him. Instead, the stress response is switched on as soon as the brain receives signals from the senses which

suggest danger.

2 The stress response is **immediate**. No matter how relaxed you are, if the brain receives signals which imply danger, the stress response is switched on and you feel alert and tense immediately. We have all experienced the situation when you are lying dozing in bed at night when you hear a noise downstairs and in a split second you are wide awake, ears 'pinned back' and heart racing.

3 It is very **powerful**. As you can see even from the simplified description above, the stress response involves major changes in the body's system and these changes cannot be simply switched off again. In our examples and in your own experience even when a straightforward threatening event is over, it takes quite some time to calm down. This is because the stress response has altered the body's level of arousal to help the person either fight or flee from danger. In a sense we are charged up for action and even when we have dealt with the threat we still have excess (surplus) energy and so we often feel shaky and emotional.

WHY DO WE HAVE THE STRESS RESPONSE AND HOW DOES IT RELATE TO ANXIETY?

In the two examples, (a) and (b) described previously you can see that in both cases the stress response was very important in terms of helping each person escape from the danger which was threatening them. However, we have also seen that the stress response is very easily and quickly triggered off and frequently is triggered off **inappropriately**, preparing our bodies for a danger that is not physical, but which threatens our self-esteem or pride for example. Why then do we have such a strong response which is so easily triggered?

The answer to this question lies in the evolution of human beings. Archaeological records of humans go back several million years. However, it is only relatively recently, within the last few thousand years that our social life has developed in such a way that we now live in large urban communities, villages, towns and cities. Before this, for many thousands of years, life was far more precarious and human beings were at the mercy of a very hostile environment on a daily basis, a hostile environment that involved continuing threats from wild animals, other humans and so on. Over those thousand of years those people who were most able to react to danger in a way which helped them escape from that danger, or fight that danger effectively, were much more likely to survive and so pass on this ability to their offspring. In this way the stress response developed so that all people were and are able to respond speedily, powerfully and immediately to any threat of physical danger, a threat which was **ever present** for our ancestors. Researchers have also named this stress response the 'fight or flight syndrome' as these are the two main responses available to us when confronted by serious physical threat, we can either try to escape it, or physically fight it.

However, over the past few thousand years we have learned to control our environment so for the vast majority of us physical threat necessitating such a powerful mechanism as the stress response is relatively rare. In terms of evolution, though, a few thousand years is a tiny amount of time so looking at our development, we are little different from our ancestors who lived in danger many thousands of years ago. To put it simply, we have developed social systems which have resulted in danger being minimised (compared to our ancestors) but our bodies are still prepared for an environment in which danger is rife. Our physical evolution has not caught up with our social evolution.

Perhaps now we can see more clearly why the stress response might be triggered off in situations where it is not appropriate. If you are in a situation where you are having an argument with someone you are, in a sense, prepared to react to this argument as though it may actually threaten your safety. As the argument continues gradually your heart rate may increase (along with the other physical signs such as respiration rate), and you will also start to feel 'worked up' psychologically. Eventually as the stress response is activated you feel extremely emotional (for example, angry) and find it very hard to behave calmly and rationally; you want to **do** something because you feel so aroused. Even if you walk away you will carry on feeling worked up for some time.

To summarise this scene briefly, we are physically prone to perceiving situations to be physically threatening **when they** need not be, and of over-reacting accordingly. If you are faced with a direct physical threat or danger you have to react very quickly and powerfully in order to maximise your chances of survival; a person who literally has to 'run for their life' runs faster than someone who is running as fast as they can for reasons of sport. The difficulty, as we can see, is that in many situations which may be psychologically threatening, but which are not physically dangerous, we do not need to do anything physically, but we often respond as though we do.

PANIC ATTACKS

If the stress response is triggered in an entirely inappropriate situation (for example whilst walking around a supermarket) it will, as we've seen, lead to strong physical signs, and in this sort of situation the experience is often termed a panic attack. Panic attacks afflict many people with anxiety difficulties and cause much distress, and perhaps the main reason for this is the fact that they seem to come 'out of the blue', so are very frightening. We will look at this fear in a bit more detail in the next chapter on psychological signs, as the ways people label panic attacks often make them much worse. The main point here, however, is that panic attacks represent the strongest form of anxiety, where the stress response has been clearly triggered, and triggered in-appropriately. (Chapter 6 looks at the life experiences a person may have before they first experience anxiety difficulties which can lead to this accidental triggering.)

THE PREPAREDNESS STATE

People who are having anxiety difficulties do not necessarily experience panic attacks, instead they may experience a continual state of edginess or tension. Whenever anyone faces a difficult situation, for example an important meeting, an examination, a driving test or an interview, they are almost certain to feel nervous and tense beforehand. This experience can be thought of as the preparedness state, and like the stress response it has developed in order to help us. However, the stress response is there to help us deal with physical danger, whereas the preparedness state is there to help us deal with situations which demand a higher level of concentration than usual. A general finding from research is that a person facing a difficult situation (for example an examination) who is not at all aroused is less likely to do as well than a person who is moderately aroused. A person who is too aroused (very anxious), is also not going to do as well. In other words, in many situations we perform better if we are moderately tense. If we are not the slightest big tense, or at the opposite extreme if we are extremely tense, our performance is significantly worse. This state of preparedness or alertness is therefore a positive ability, improving our concentration and general performance. However, we can only sustain the effective preparedness state for so long. After a while we become subject to negative effects such as tiredness, sleeplessness, and irritability, with physical signs like tension headaches. Some people (for reasons explored in Chapters 5 and 6) appear to be in this preparedness state for long periods of time, in which case although they may not experience the extremes of anxiety they do feel constantly tense and on edge, and so may feel ordinary problems are much more serious than they are. It's almost as if they are continually waiting for an examination which isn't going to happen, and so they never get a chance to unwind. As we will see being in this preparedness state too long can not only bring on some of the physical signs mentioned at the beginning of this chapter, but can also make it more likely that the stress response itself is triggered off. Nevertheless it is important to keep in mind that both the stress response and the preparedness state are extremely useful mechanisms; it is when they are inappropriately triggered or kept on for too long that they lead to distress.

SUMMARY

1 There are a number of physical signs of anxiety which are caused by the activation of the **stress response.**
2 The stress response is a mechanism which all humans have; its basic function is to help us escape from or fight physical danger by causing our bodies and minds

to become very highly alert.

3 The stress response developed over thousands of years of evolution, when human beings lived in an environment in which physical danger (in the form of wild animals etc.) was ever present. It was then vital for our survival.

4 Although we do not now live in situations where there is as much danger as there was before, we still have the same stress response as our ancestors. Often, if we feel worried or threatened (but when there is no actual physical danger) the stress response is inappropriately activated and we are physically prepared to 'fight or flee' when neither response is appropriate. At its most extreme this will be experienced as a **panic attack** which appears to come 'out of the blue'.

5 Some situations may also cause us to respond so that although the full stress response is not switched on, we still become significantly more physically and mentally tense. We can call this the preparedness state.

6 The preparedness state can help us by improving our alertness and ability to concentrate. However, if we are in this state too long we may suffer some of the physical signs of anxiety as well as experiencing other difficulties like tiredness, sleeplessness and irritability.

PROBE QUESTIONNAIRE

The physical signs of anxiety:
1 List those physical signs you experienced last time the full stress response was switched on.

2 List those physical signs you experienced the last time you were in the preparedness state.

③ The psychological side of anxiety

The psychological side of anxiety is the most complex of the three sides, and the least well understood. For this reason it is important to see how the different sorts of experiences that come under the heading of 'the psychological side of anxiety' relate together. These experiences can be seen as coming under one or other of the three following psychological areas:

1 The **emotions** or **feelings** people have when they are anxious
2 The specific things people **think** or say to themselves when they are anxious
3 The underlying **attitudes** people have which may help bring on and/or maintain anxiety

These three areas often overlap very closely, and in fact can be impossible to separate at times. However, it is useful to distinguish between the three as this can be crucial when learning to deal with anxiety.

We will look at each of the three areas in turn, before relating them to each other.

THE FIRST AREA OF THE PSYCHOLOGICAL SIDE OF ANXIETY: THE THINGS PEOPLE FEEL WHEN ANXIOUS

This area deals with the **emotions** people experience. Examples of the strongest sort of feelings people experience are as follows:

1 Feeling frightened or panicky
2 Feeling that you are losing control
3 Feeling that fear is going to 'take over'
4 Feeling very emotional without being able to 'pin down' the emotion.

Examples of milder states of emotion include:

5 Irritability
6 'Edginess'
7 Nervousness

In order to help us see where the strongest feelings come from we can look back at the stress response. As we can see the essential function of the stress response is to help us deal with physical danger, and to do this a lot of bodily changes are brought into action. However, there would be no point in being **physically** prepared for action without being emotionally aroused as well. We need to be emotionally aroused in order to motivate us to deal with danger. The sense of **fear** therefore makes us want to **do** something, and our bodies are activated to do that something very powerfully. In practice the complex actions of hormones not only affect the body, they also affect the feelings or emotional state as well. As mentioned in Chapter 2, if a person is injected with the hormone adrenaline, he or she will feel physically 'worked up'. He or she will also feel more **emotional**. The emotion need not necessarily be specific—for example anger or fear—rather, the hormone works by increasing the general **emotionality**. If you inject people with adrenaline and them put them into a situation which is mildly physically threatening, they are likely to feel intense feelings of fear. If you put them in a situation which is mildly irritating (for example someone pushing in front of them in a queue) they will feel **anger**. Injecting someone with adrenaline is obviously artificial, but the general point is that the stress response works by increasing the general **emotionality** of a person (as well as preparing that person to deal physically with danger) and this emotionality makes that person want to **do** something.

If you think back to the last time you felt emotional in this way, you may find it difficult to accurately describe what it is you felt. We have words like 'anger' and 'fear' but often when we feel emotional it is difficult to label the feeling this clearly.

This is even more the case at the milder levels of feelings experienced at lower levels of anxiety. Here the main experience may be of irritability or nervousness or simply never being able to relax. A person can be in the preparedness state for so long that he or she doesn't even really notice. One effect of being in this state is that real problems are likely to produce an exaggerated response, so a relatively trivial incident—for example a minor car accident—may lead to quite disproportionate feelings of anger and upset.

To summarise the emotional area of anxiety: the main reason for the major increases in emotionality that accompany the higher levels of anxiety is that it motivates us to do something about the threat which has produced the increase in anxiety. At lower levels of anxiety the main reason for the milder degree of emotionality is to improve concentration and general alertness. In both cases the problem is that these states of emotionality can be produced when there is no threat, or when there is no external reason for being in a high state of alertness. In these cases the person experiencing the emotionality will try and label his or her experiences in order to make sense of them. This brings us to the second area of the psychological side of anxiety.

THE SECOND AREA OF THE PSYCHOLOGICAL SIDE OF ANXIETY: THE SPECIFIC THINGS PEOPLE THINK WHEN ANXIOUS

Again we can start by looking at some examples of the things people often think to themselves, particularly when they are experiencing higher levels of anxiety, and especially if they experience panic attacks seemingly 'out of the blue'.

1 I must be going mad
2 I can't cope with these feelings
3 There must be something seriously wrong with me
4 I'm going to make a complete fool of myself
5 I'm going to lose control
6 I'm going to have a nervous breakdown if this carries on
7 I must be having a heart attack
8 I must have a brain tumour or something
9 I'll end up in a mental hospital

(These are only a few examples of the things people think to themselves; at the end of this chapter in the probe questionnaire you will be asked to note down those things you often think to yourself when anxious.)

The main point of looking at the things people specifically think when they are anxious is that these thoughts often serve to worsen the anxiety experience. We will look at an example to illustrate this:

Jane Smith is standing in the wings of the stage waiting for her cue to go on. It is her first role in the amateur dramatic company play and there are a lot of people out there waiting. She feels her heart racing and she is breathing very quickly. She feels quite shaky.

(a) she thinks about how excited she is and thinks how good it will be to get on to the stage and get into the part she has been rehearsing. She imagines how relieved and cheerful everyone will be at the end.

or

(b) she thinks how frightened she is and imagines walking onto the stage and forgetting her lines. She thinks about how embarrassing it would be having to face everybody afterwards. She starts to feel desperate at the idea.

The physical signs start off the same in both (a) and (b). The difference is in the things she is thinking. In (a) she has labelled the signs as meaning that she is 'excited'. This leads her to think about the play in a very positive way and she goes on to imagine how well things are going. However, in (b) she labels the signs as 'fear'. This leads her to imagine things going wrong and all the negative consequences that would happen. This gives the 'feeling' of anxiety that desperate, almost depressed edge.

This example shows how the things that a person thinks— often without being particularly aware of what he or she is doing—can significantly intensify the feelings of anxiety. Looking back at the list of things people think, you can see that each one is likely to have the effect of worsening the anxiety. If you're feeling anxious for whatever reason, and if you then start to think that you might be going mad, you're going to feel even more panicky.

A second, related effect of having these kinds of thoughts is that they can bring to the surface of the mind related memories. Look back at the example of Jane Smith. In (a) she labelled her feelings as being due to excitement, and she went on to imagine doing well in the performance. What also happened when Jane did this was that she made more accessible all the positive memories she had of similar situations when she felt excited. Every person has many millions of related memories, flavoured with positive, negative or neutral feelings. When we are having a good experience, we can more easily remember good times like the ones we are having; those complex and often inter-related memories rise to the surface of our minds, and even if we do not actually recall them consciously, they still may unconsciously improve our mood or our feelings. Similarly, negative thoughts and negative experiences bring to the surface of consciousness (or just below the surface) other negative memories which in turn worsen our mood. This is what happened to Jane Smith in (b). She imagined going on to the stage and forgetting her lines. Like all of us she has had times in the past where she has been in similar situations, such as 'drying up' when in the middle of saying something important to someone. This sort of memory is activated by negative thoughts, which then increase the negative feeling and intensify the anxiety. All this can happen without our being aware of the subtle things going on inside our minds. If we again look back at the list of examples of the specific thoughts people have, it is not hard to imagine how the memories and feelings likely to be associated with them may well have a powerful effect on the anxiety level of the person experiencing them. Someone who is thinking 'I am going to lose control' is probably activating all sorts of negative memories of previous times when he or she felt out of control in situations.

AUTOMATIC THOUGHTS

Some thoughts can occur so often that they become virtually automatic, and it is particularly important that a person engaging in automatic negative ways of thinking becomes aware of them so he or she can change them. An automatic thought such as 'I can't cope with this' may have developed over a long period of time, so that the person is not really aware of thinking it; rather, it is a background idea which, as we saw above, activates other negative memories and influences feelings. Automatic thoughts can be so long-standing that they are fairly deeply embedded in the way a person looks at things, and this will overlap with the third area, that of **attitudes**.

To summarise the area of specific things people think when anxious: when a person is experiencing physical signs of anxiety, along with the emotional feelings of fear, that person is likely to think of their experience in very negative terms, particularly if he or she does not understand it. Thoughts such as 'I must be going mad' will inevitably serve to worsen the feelings. In addition, negative thoughts can summon up negative **memories**, of which the person might not be **consciously** aware, but which still affect their feelings negatively. Sometimes thoughts may be so long-term that they become virtually automatic. The person uses them without being particularly aware of doing so; the automatic thought provides the 'background' on which other thoughts are overlaid.

THE THIRD AREA OF THE PSYCHOLOGICAL SIDE OF ANXIETY: THE ATTITUDES A PERSON HAS WHICH MAY HELP BRING ON AND/OR MAINTAIN ANXIETY

This is the most complex area of the psychological side of anxiety, and one in which many different approaches have been developed in order to try and help our understanding. The reading list at the end of this book gives a few books which deal with this area in more detail, so for our purposes here we will look at some of the more obvious attitudes which are often involved in people's experience of anxiety.

Before describing what these attitudes are, we will look at an example in order to illustrate how particular attitudes can affect people:

Alan Johnson is a salesman working in computing. He is very good at his job and is well thought of by his colleagues. However, he feels in a continual state of tension at work. When he is with a potential client discussing a sale he feels very tense, experiencing physical sensations like increased heart rate, increased respiration and so on. These feelings become very bad if he does not win the order and he feels a complete failure. Every salesman feels disappointed when they fail to make a sale, but with Alan Johnson it is far worse than this. He takes any 'failure' to make a sale (which is bound to happen quite often) to mean that he is a failure. This means that he is likely to feel 'under threat' for much of his time at work, hence his continual feelings of anxiety. Now, if we look at the things Alan is thinking we may find that there are a few anxiety-provoking thoughts, but what seems to be creating the physical feelings of anxiety and the emotional experience of anxiety is his **attitude** to situations at work. It is **as if** he is saying these things to himself:

'If I do not win this order I am a complete failure'
'I must succeed every time'
'Failure is unforgivable'

An attitude in this sense, then, is a set of beliefs which a person may not be aware of, but which influence the way he or she sees situations. So, although the person may not be saying things to him or herself, the attitude can be seen to be equivalent to one or more statements about him or her. In other words, an attitude affects the way someone approaches a situation through acting as if he or she were saying specific things to him or herself.

People who develop anxiety problems sometimes have attitudes which may serve to worsen that anxiety, or keep it going. The difficulty with recognising anxiety-provoking attitudes is the fact that we are often not aware of them. This is because our attitudes, the way we look at ourselves and the rest of the world, develop from a very early age. As we grow older, they become increasingly 'unconscious', so we tend not to notice their effects.

Obviously attitudes are highly complex, but there do seem to be a few which are particularly relevant to anxiety. For example, many women are brought up to believe that the woman's place is 'in the home' and that a woman's main duty is to look after the needs of husband, children and home, sometimes at the expense of looking after her own needs. If she does not do this she may feel she is a 'failure'. This sort of attitude can lead to anxiety for many reasons. For example, if the woman wants to go to work, or perhaps if she has to go to work for economic reasons, she may well feel pressure or strain due to guilt. As well as this, women in paid employment may often end up doing as much housework, cooking etc., as they would do if they did not have a paid job. (The husband's attitude towards sharing these jobs may often worsen matters of course.)

Whatever, the effect of this sort of attitude may be to increase the amount of stress the woman experiences (we will look at stress in more detail in Chapter 6) leading to the experience of anxiety.

In a similar way, men are generally brought up to be competitive in many situations, and tied in with this is the widespread attitude that men should not show vulnerability. If a man expresses his emotional needs, for example by crying, this is seen as 'weakness' and he may feel less of a man because of this. This expectation that men should not show their more vulnerable side is so widespread that a man may find it hard to even identify when he is feeling emotionally 'needy'. Instead of being able to express that need honestly and directly, he may 'back off' and become more distant. Deep down he is frightened of what would happen if he did say how he felt, so his solution is to deny his feelings.

We can look at the example of Alan Johnson in a bit more depth to illustrate this. As a child and young man his parents, his father in particular, had been critical of him if he was ever less than best at everything. He unconsciously carried this attitude over into his adult life and, as the attitude in this case was highly unrealistic and rigid, he often experienced quite intense feelings of anxiety, particularly when confronted with failure. Because of the general attitude that it is wrong for men to express these intense feelings of self-doubt, he was not able to discuss his feelings with his wife; instead he withdrew from her, showing signs of irritability and anger instead, so his anxiety at work continued to seriously disrupt his life.

Here is another example:

Susan Brown is a young woman who feels extremely anxious in social situations. She feels panicky and is preoccupied with thoughts that people are looking at her, and that they are thinking that there is something wrong with her, that she is inadequate in some way. She is not very big, and feels particularly self-conscious about being thin. She comes from a large family where she is one of the youngest: her brothers and sisters were big and boisterous so she felt intimidated by the rest of the family. Her parents often

B

argued—sometimes violently—and this increased her feeling of insecurity. Generally, although she was part of a big lively family, she always felt under threat and rarely felt confident enough to express herself assertively. Therefore, her attitudes to herself tended to be very negative: she saw herself as being useless and as having nothing to say to people. Her attitude to other people was that she tended to feel very threatened by them and social situations, therefore, seemed particularly anxiety-provoking. She focussed her feelings very much on her size: she felt that if only she were bigger she would feel far more confident and feel much more positive about herself.

Just as Alan's difficulties stemmed from attitudes he absorbed from his parents (he felt he had to succeed) and from society generally (it is wrong for men to show their emotions) so Susan Brown's attitudes stemmed not just from her experiences in her family, but from society as well. In this case Susan experienced a general pressure that she should **look** a certain way. All around her she noticed images on television, in advertising and so on, as to how women should look and behave, and she felt herself to be quite inadequate compared to these (false) ideas about what women should be. This pressure to conform to unrealistic images of women affects all women, but in Susan's case it was particularly powerful as she already has a tendency to see herself negatively due to her experiences in her family.

We will look at Susan Brown's story again in Chapter 8, but it is worth making the point at this stage that her pre-occupation with her thinness—reflecting as it does on the deeper negative attitudes towards herself—should not be the target of assistance: rather, it should be the attitude itself. Instead she would need to learn—through positive experiences—to see herself as being more personally effective, to gradually build her confidence, in the expectation that this change in attitude would eventually not only help the anxiety, but also lead to her concern about her size becoming weakened so it no longer caused her to be preoccupied by it.

Similarly with Alan Johnson, in order for him to deal with his anxiety, he would first need to acknowledge the deep feelings of fear of failure, and then gradually learn to express his fears openly, rather than running away from these feelings.

To summarise this third area of the psychological scale of anxiety: we develop our attitudes starting from the earliest times of our lives, and they receive influences from many sources, from our immediate family (parents in particular) to society generally. Some attitudes can lead us to be particularly prone to perceiving situations in ways which create anxiety, and the difficulty is that as these attitudes are so long-standing we tend to be unaware of them. In this case it is important to develop a degree of awareness of these attitudes, in order to do something about them.

HOW THE THREE AREAS OF THE PSYCHOLOGICAL SIDE OF ANXIETY RELATE TOGETHER

The main way the three areas relate together is through **reinforcing** each other. For example, a woman who has negative attitudes towards herself in some ways is more likely to engage in negative thoughts. These, in turn, will set off negative associations and she may start experiencing particularly strong feelings of anxiety. As we will see in Chapter 5, anxiety can be set off through the specific stresses a person experiences. In this case negative thoughts following the experience of anxiety can give rise to negative memories and attitudes. This again worsens mood, and so a vicious circle is set in motion: negative anxiety-related feelings, thoughts and attitudes all reinforcing each other, so the feelings of anxiety are experienced as if they dominate the whole of the person's world. This vicious circle can be largely outside the person's awareness, and so recognising its existence is very important in terms of planning how to deal with it. In Chapter 8 we will look at ways of breaking down this vicious circle in more detail.

SUMMARY

We can split the psychological side of anxiety into three overlapping areas:

   1 The feelings a person has

2 The specific thoughts a person has

3 The attitudes a person has

1 The feelings of anxiety at their strongest are experienced as panic. This is a direct consequence of the 'switching on' of the stress response, whose function is not only to make us physically prepared for danger, but emotionally prepared to do something about the danger. The milder feelings of anxiety, which include irritability and nervousness are a consequence of being in the preparedness state where we experience a raised arousal level in order to help us deal more effectively with non-dangerous situations. Both these states can be relatively easily produced without there necessarily being an external trigger.

2 If a person is experiencing these feelings of anxiety, he or she is particularly likely to start engaging in negative thinking. This serves to directly worsen the anxiety. Negative thoughts can also trigger off other negative feelings and memories (possibly unconsciously) to further intensify anxiety-related moods. Some thoughts are so long-standing that they tend to be automatic.

3 Attitudes are influenced from many sources, from our parents to society generally, and start forming from the earliest time in our lives. They can lead us to develop ways of looking at the world which help to create feelings of anxiety. Marked negative attitudes to ourselves are particularly likely to lead to feelings of anxiety in various situations.

These three areas overlap considerably, and each tends to reinforce the other, and this reinforcement often tends to be outside our consciousness. We need to develop enough awareness of each area to be able to see that this mutual reinforcement is taking place, before going on to break it down.

PROBE QUESTIONNAIRE

1 Describe the particular feelings you get when tense or anxious.

2 Think of the last time you felt particularly anxious,

and note down as accurately as possible the specific things you **thought** to yourself. Try to recall any memories of similar situations these thoughts triggered off.

3 **Attitudes.** This is a difficult question, but try to describe beliefs and attitudes which you may be more aware of now, which may be involved in your experience of anxiety. It may be useful to think back to earlier experiences you had which may have led to you developing attitudes which could create anxiety feelings. Also it would be useful to write a brief description of yourself which you imagine someone close to you, someone who knows you very well, might write. Does this give you any clues as to anxiety-creating attitudes you have?

4 When you have done this, try to work out ways in which these three areas **reinforce** each other.

4 The behavioural side of anxiety

So far we have looked at how anxiety affects people physically and psychologically. The third and final side of anxiety is the way it affects what people **do**, how they actually behave.

Anxiety can affect people's behaviour in many different ways, but perhaps the most common is **avoidance**. Avoidance comes in many forms; here are just a few:

1 Avoiding social situations such as pubs, restaurants, meetings
2 Avoiding going out; staying in the 'safety' of the home instead
3 Making excuses not to do things
4 Avoiding facing up to certain people who make you feel anxious
5 Avoiding public transport; relying on lifts or walking
6 Not standing up for yourself in situations when you know you should

(There are many other examples that could be given, but think now about the main things you avoid. At the end of this chapter there is a questionnaire and you can note down which situations you avoid.)

Other things people **do** because of anxiety include the following:

7 Using tranquillisers or alcohol as props to help in facing situations
8 Only going out when accompanied
9 Always sitting near the exits in cinemas, etc.

PROBLEMS WITH AVOIDANCE

People avoid situations in order to avoid feeling anxiety. Sometimes they do it so well they never feel anxious. For example, Richard Smith is afraid of flying. He is not generally anxious (no more than most people) but whenever he gets near an aeroplane his stomach starts churning, his heart races, his legs feel 'like jelly', he feels petrified and imagines the plane crashing killing all the passengers. Now, if he never needs to use an aeroplane, then he can avoid ever experiencing that anxiety. In other words, in this case, his **avoidance behaviour** does not interfere with his life.

Denis Long is a fitter who experiences various anxiety signs whenever he goes to the works' canteen or other social situations. He starts to avoid these situations but finds that the more he avoids them, the worse it gets. He soon starts to feel anxious at tea breaks, or at any time when he is not directly working and has to sit with other colleagues. He eventually starts to take time off 'sick' in order to avoid the anxiety.

In this case then, Denis Long's avoidance behaviour significantly affects his life as the (social) situations he will not face up to are a crucial part of his day-to-day existence. We can also see that once he started to avoid one situation, he then started to avoid others. This is a feature of avoidance behaviour: once you start to avoid situations because of anxiety, you are likely to start to avoid other, similar situations.

A second, related problem with avoidance is that once you avoid a situation it becomes harder to face the second time. For example:

Mary Williams is a teacher. Each Friday she has to teach a particularly difficult group of children and this causes her a considerable amount of anxiety, particularly the night before. One Friday she decided she just couldn't face them and so telephones the school to say she was sick. However, the following week she found she started to worry and feel anxious about the class from the very beginning of the week, whereas previously she would start to worry the night before.

This generally happens once a person has allowed anxiety to make them avoid a situation: it becomes more difficult to face the next time and so the person is more likely to avoid it **again** and the pattern continues.

The third main result of avoidance behaviour is the effect it has on a person's confidence. If you avoid a situation you may feel relieved that you do not have to face it. However, you will also feel guilty and probably a bit of a failure. In other words avoidance can reduce your self-esteem and make you feel emotionally 'low'. (The opposite occurs when you make yourself face up to situations. Even if you have felt anxious during that situation when it is over you are glad you did it and you also feel a **boost** to your confidence.) The fourth effect of avoidance is related to the third. Put simply: people avoid situations which cause them anxiety, but sometimes these situations are also an important source of **pleasure** for people as well. By avoiding situations that once were a source of pleasure, people can risk becoming depressed.

Julie Green had for various reasons begun to experience quite bad anxiety signs in confined social situations. She had enjoyed going to the local pub with a few friends several times a week. When she started feeling panicky at the pub, she made excuses to her friends and stopped going altogether. She missed these outings with her friends and felt very despondent on those evenings when she used to go out. Gradually she become despondent at other times, feeling so tied down by the anxiety that she eventually began to feel quite badly depressed much of the time.

AVOIDANCE AND SELF-CONFIDENCE

The general result of avoidance is that it can gradually but significantly reduce a person's self-confidence or self-esteem. Our level of self-confidence is really much more vulnerable or precarious than we often think; it often doesn't take much to lose self-confidence. In terms of the behavioural side of anxiety avoidance can be particularly powerful in decreasing a person's self-confidence. This is particularly the case if a person is avoiding **social** situations, as the most important source of our self-esteem is through our relationships with other people.

PROBLEMS WITH RELATING TO PEOPLE

Imagine you are waiting in a queue in a post office when someone walks up and pushes in front of you. Would you:

(a) get very cross and angrily tell them to get to the back of the queue
(b) feel and look cross but say nothing
(c) politely ask them if they would join the end of the queue?

If we look at (a) it is certainly 'actively standing up for your rights' but it is also rather aggressive in the sense that the anger is out of proportion to the situation, and is likely to produce a negative response from the person addressed in that way.

Option (b) is under-assertive. If you have been in that situation you will probably remember feeling cross and embarrassed. More importantly you will also have perhaps felt a bit 'feeble', a bit of a failure for having allowed the person to push in like that.

The third response, (c), is probably the best; it is assertive (actually standing up for your rights) but it is also polite. In other words, you do not try to make the other person look foolish (it is not a serious matter after all) and this makes it easy for them to apologise and go to the end of the queue.

We can therefore distinguish three very general ways of responding to situations like this:

1 aggression
2 passivity
3 assertion

Aggressive responses may 'frighten' someone into doing what you want them to, but at the risk of the situation becoming necessarily tense and unpleasant. Sometimes the other person feels they can only respond by being aggressive back, for the sake of their 'pride', so a trivial situation escalates into a serious one.

Passive responses make a person more likely to take advantage again, but most importantly leave you feeling angry with the person and angry with yourself. Your self-esteem is significantly eroded.

Assertive responses are usually the most effective. Politely standing up for your rights is less likely to 'threaten' someone and so allows them to 'save their face'. More importantly it leaves you feeling pleased that you stood up for yourself, increasing your self-esteem.

These three sorts of behavioural response can involve anxiety in many ways: aggressive responses are likely to turn ordinary situations into difficult, stressful ones, causing anxiety to all concerned; passive responses lead to loss of self-esteem and makes a person much more likely to feel anxious; standing up for oneself by being assertive can cause anxiety but it is, in the long term, the most useful way of dealing with situations in terms of a person's self-confidence.

Aggression, passivity and assertion are closely linked with attitudes, so in Chapters 8 and 9 in Part Two we will look at the ways people behave toward others in more detail.

Generally, the behavioural side of anxiety is the one which can interfere with a person's life most, as the most frequent response is to **avoid** situations in different ways. At its most extreme, people sometimes avoid virtually all social situations, leading to severe effects on self-confidence. Perhaps most importantly, people can never learn how to **deal** with anxiety whilst avoiding the situations in which it occurs.

SUMMARY

The behavioural side of anxiety usually consists of people avoiding situations where they feel they would experience the physical and psychological signs of anxiety. The way people relate to others is also involved.

Avoidance causes four problems:

1 Once you regularly avoid one situation, there is a risk that you end up avoiding other situations which are similar.
2 If you avoid a situation, it can become harder to face the next time.
3 When you avoid something, although the initial feeling may be relief at not having to face it, the longer term effect is that you lose confidence and feel a failure.
4 People who avoid situations, especially social situations, may also avoid important sources of enjoyment, so risk becoming depressed.

The overall effect of avoidance is that the **pattern** of a person's life is disrupted; he or she stops doing things which may have once been very important, and the loss of self-confidence that follows can be very powerful. People may also behave towards others in ways which can create anxiety. Passive or aggressive ways of responding are particularly likely to be involved in the experience of anxiety. Passive behaviour especially can lead to the low self-confidence that often creates states of anxiety.

PROBE QUESTIONNAIRE

1 Write down in detail how the anxiety you experience affects your behaviour: what you actually do in situations if you experience anxiety.

2 Write down in detail all those situations you actively avoid.

3 Think about the ways you behave towards stress at home, at work and socially. Write down examples of things you do with people based on the three sorts of responses: aggressive, passive and assertive.

5 Anxiety: why me? Stressful life events and life strains

Now we have looked at the three sides of anxiety, quite a few questions should have been answered. However, if you do have anxiety difficulties, one of the most pressing questions is 'Why Me?', so in this chapter we will look at the things that happen to people that can lead to them becoming anxious. Before we do this, it is important to bear in mind one of the points made in Chapter 2, that is, that the stress response is a **normal** and **necessary** part of human functioning. What we are going to look at now is how it can be 'switched on' when it is not really required.

STRESSFUL LIFE EVENTS AND LIFE STRAINS

The terms 'stressful life events' and 'life strains' were first coined by researchers studying the reasons why people become psychologically distressed, depressed in particular, from the point of view of looking at things that had happened to them in their lives **before** they became depressed. In other words, they were looking at the sorts of experiences (such as losing a job, suffering a bereavement) that could lead to a person becoming depressed. Although this research is now just beginning with people who experience anxiety rather than depression, there are several possibilities we can suggest why anxiety difficulties people experience are **brought on** by experiences they had previously, experiences we can describe as life events and life strains.

STRESSFUL LIFE EVENTS

For our purposes here, a stressful life event is basically an experience a person has which significantly changes or disrupts his or her life. Life events may be either negative (such as losing one's job) or positive (such as getting married), although people who experience anxiety are more likely to have experienced a **negative** life event previously.

The following list contains some of the experiences people may have which may be significant life events:

1 Suffering a short term illness
2 Having a bad accident
3 Being made redundant
4 Having a child
5 Getting married
6 Suffering the breakdown of a relationship
7 Having someone close to you become ill
8 Having someone close to you dying
9 Having to sit important examinations
10 Moving house
11 Changing job (including being demoted or promoted)
12 Retiring

We all experience life events like these throughout our lives, without necessarily experiencing stress as a result. However, it is possible that these kinds of experience lead to increased levels of tension which may lead to anxiety, and we will look at why this is the case later in this chapter.

LIFE STRAINS

The second sort of stress a person may experience is due to **life strain.**

Life strains are similar to stressful life events, in that they increase the general level of physical tension. The difference is that life events tend to be 'one-off', in the sense that something happens to you **once,** whereas life strains are experiences that result in **continuous** tension. Here are a few examples of life strains:

1 Being unemployed
2 Being physically unwell
3 Experiencing continuous serious relationship problems (with members of one's family or with close friends)
4 Experiencing pressure at work
5 Suffering severe financial hardship
6 Experiencing chronic boredom

Again these are just a few examples, and people vary in how much they are affected by such strains.

There is an overlap between life strains and life events. For example, a person may suffer an acute physical illness which is treated and **cured** over a relatively short period of time (for example appendicitis). This illness is quickly cured, it is a 'one-off' life **event**. However, if there were physical complications leading to the person requiring long-term medical treatment, then this sort of problem can be seen as a life **strain**, significantly affecting day-to-day life.

Importantly, stressful life events can lead to serious life strains. Perhaps the most important example of this is redundancy and unemployment. People who experience the life event of redundancy are more likely than others to develop anxiety problems, even if they manage to find another job quite quickly. The shock of losing one's job can be enough in itself to cause anxiety difficulties. However, if that person cannot find another job, then not only will he or she have to cope with the effects of the life event losing the job, but also with the life strain caused by unemployment, which will probably involve (amongst other things) additional financial hardship, social stigma, boredom and so on.

In addtion, for someone suffering financial hardship each day is likely to comprise severe problems of how to manage; in a sense buying each meal may become a mini-stressful life event in itself.

Problems with relationships are similar. A person may suffer the traumatic event of a relationship with his or her partner splitting up. That in itself may well be quite a significant blow. However, if he or she has few or no friends to rely on for support, then that will lead to a significant life strain: loneliness.

HOW DO LIFE EVENTS AND LIFE STRAINS AFFECT PEOPLE?

This is a very complex question, and a complete answer to it is still far off. However, there are tentative suggestions which can be made.

Life events and life strains can be seen as affecting people in two related ways:

1 They have an effect on their overall **physical** level of tension

2 They may have an effect on them **psychologically**, through affecting their level of self-esteem or self-confidence

These two are related, but initially we'll take each in turn.

THE PHYSICAL EFFECTS OF LIFE EVENTS AND LIFE STRAINS

To help show these effects, look at Figure 5.1. This is a highly simplified view of stress and anxiety. The vertical line

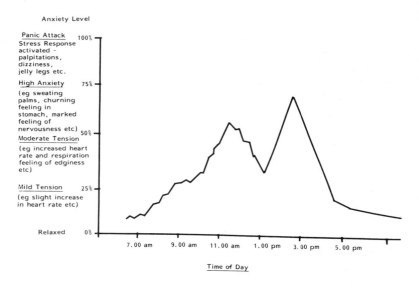

Fig. 5.1

on the left represents anxiety level. To make this more easily understood, there are percentages for different levels of anxiety, starting at 0% and going up to 100%. As the anxiety level increases, you can see that signs of anxiety gradually increase, until at 100% the person experiences a full-scale panic attack, with palpitations, feelings of extreme fear, etc.

The horizontal line along the bottom of this diagram represents a twelve hour period in a single day. The jagged line above represents an imaginary person's typical anxiety level as it changes throughout the day. For this example we'll assume this person is a woman, Denise Smith, who is a teacher with no particular anxiety problem. We'll assume also that we've assessed her physical level of tension by taking various measurements regularly throughout the day, measurements that tell us how anxious she is, such as her heart rate, her breathing rate, her level of muscle tension, the amount of adrenaline in her blood stream and so on.

Looking at the diagram you can see that her level of anxiety changes quite a lot; she is fairly relaxed on waking up (10% anxiety level), but there are two peaks, one at 11 a.m. (55% anxiety level) and one at 2.30 p.m. (65% anxiety level).

As a teacher, she sometimes has difficult large classes to deal with, and if she has one at 11 a.m. and one at 2.30 p.m. we should not be surprised to see that her anxiety level 'peaks' at those times. However, there is an important point to look at here: her level of anxiety reaches 65% on diagram, but although she may feel 'tense' and 'on edge' she does not particularly **notice** the increases in the various physical signs of anxiety. So although, for example, her heart rate may increase significantly, from the relaxed level when she woke to the increased level when she is standing in front of her 'difficult' class at 11 a.m., she is **not** really aware of it. This is very important because it illustrates the fact that at low and medium levels of anxiety we tend to be unaware of how tense or anxious we are. Looking at Figure 5.1 we can see that it is only at quite **high** levels of anxiety that the physical symptoms are noticeable, such as severe muscular tension, palpitations, strong feelings of fear and so on. (Having said that, if our teacher stayed at 50% all day without going much below or above, then she would probably experience towards the end of the day signs like exhaustion, headaches, etc., so we'll discuss this aspect later on.)

It is very likely that this picture of anxiety levels, simplified though it is, is relevant for virtually everybody; we all vary throughout the day in our levels of tension, and for the most part we are unaware of how tense we are except at moderately high levels, when we are aware of feeling 'on edge' or irritable, etc.

The next step is to show how life events and life strains affect this anxiety level. Look at Figure 5.2. The difference between this and Figure 5.1 is that the horizontal line is now in **days** whereas the other was in **hours**. The vertical line (anxiety level) stays the same.

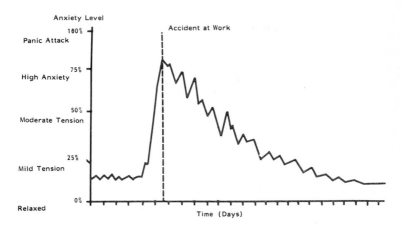

Fig. 5.2

Our example this time is Alan Jones who is an electrician working in a large factory. We can see that although his overall anxiety level fluctuates a fair degree it averages out at about 20% until the point (marked by the dotted line) at which he was involved in a fairly bad accident at work when a piece of machinery overbalanced and fell, narrowly missing him. Although he was not injured himself, a workmate of his was badly hurt and Alan had to help look after him until the ambulance came. We can see from this diagram that, naturally enough, as well as being upset for his workmate, he also became more tense physically, up to 75% on the scale. Although this tension gradually diminished, it was over two weeks before it went down to its previous level, despite the fact that this stress for Alan Jones himself was not particularly severe. Another point, if we look at the diagram again, is that after the stress, not only was Alan's level higher, it fluctuated quite widely as well (that is, after the stress his tension level was quite unstable, going up and down). In terms of his emotions this would result in his feeling okay one minute and very 'edgy' the next. This is similar to the preparedness state described in Chapter 2.

We could say, in fact, that during this period he was particularly **vulnerable** to the effects of further stress or strain. For example, let us assume that two weeks after that accident, Alan's mother is rushed to hospital with a heart attack. This is obviously going to cause him much distress, and if we look at Figure 5.3 we can see that this second

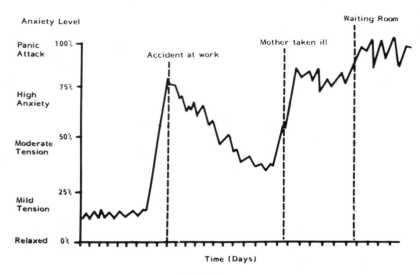

Fig. 5.3

stressful life event happens before he has fully recovered from the effects of the last (although as far as he is concerned, he had got over it). In other words, he was not aware of his vulnerability to further stress.

The second vertical dotted line on this diagram shows how this second event increases his tension level to around 80%. Alan then will be aware of not only feeling emotionally upset at his mother's illness, but feeling very worked up physically as well. At this point you can see that Alan's anxiety level is very high; in fact it is so high that it will only take a small **further** increase in tension to reach a level where the full stress response is switched on and he will experience a panic attack. Let us imagine that this occurs while he is in the dentist's waiting room a week after his mother was taken ill. This sort of situation would cause most of us to feel a bit more tense than usual. However, as we can see,

Alan's level is so high before he even sets foot in the waiting room, that this small increase in tension sets off the stress response (marked by the third vertical dotted line in Figure 5.3).

In terms of the impact on Alan, the following happens:

He is sitting in the waiting room feeling tense and edgy, wishing that the receptionist would hurry up and call his name to go in. Suddenly, and apparently 'out of the blue', he feels his heart pounding, he feels hot and dizzy and very frightened. He feels he has to get out of the waiting room, and he rushes out. Outside he feels very shaky, but is still very frightened. He has no idea what happened to him and he wonders whether, if he had stayed in the waiting room, he would have had a heart attack or a stroke.

We can predict with Alan that because he does not understand what has happened to him, it would be quite easy for the **fear** of the anxiety attack to lead to him experiencing it again. His 'fear of fear' leads to him avoiding social situations similar to the waiting room. In the next chapter we will look at how this takes place in more detail, but we can see from this example how the stressful life events Alan experienced eventually led to the triggering of the stress response, the physical signs of which we discussed in Chapter 2. Not understanding what was happening to him led to the psychological signs of anxiety we discussed in Chapter 3, which eventually led to the behavioural signs—primarily avoidance—discussed in Chapter 4.

In the example of Alan Jones we looked at the impact of stressful life events on a person's level of tension. We can also look at an example of a life strain on a person's level of tension. To do this let us go back to our first example of Denise Smith, the teacher. She is married with two teenage children (enough of a stress in itself!). Then her elderly frail mother comes to live near Denise and comes to rely on her for many things, company, physical care and so on. Over the months it is not hard to imagine that the life strain of looking after her mother, looking after her family (she gets some, but not sufficient help from her husband) as well as holding down a demanding job, leads to a steady and significant increase in her level of tension.

Figure 5.4 is similar to Figure 5.1 except that there is a second dotted line above the original one. This second lines

Anxiety Level

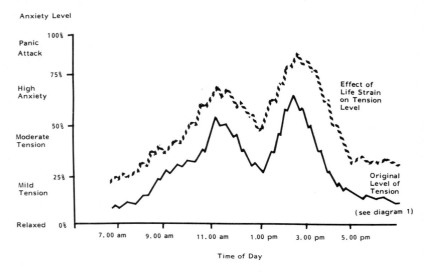

Fig. 5.4

illustrates the effect on Denise's level of physical tension of the life strain of looking after her mother.

The second line is very similar to the original one, but it is shifted up a significant extent. If we look at those classes which originally caused Denise to be moderately tense at work, we can see that they now produce very high levels of tension. In fact, it would not be surprising that, if the difficult class was particularly disruptive one day, this further increase in tension might lead to the triggering of the stress response and she would experience similar physical sensations to Alan Jones in the waiting room, as well as experiencing the same urge to rush out of the class. If she did so, and if she then started to avoid classes, we can imagine that this anxiety problem would cause a serious disruption to her life.

This example shows how life strains can lead to a gradual (often unnoticed) increase in tension, sometimes over a long period of time. This increase in tension will make that person particularly vulnerable to the effects of day-to-day stresses (as in the example of Denise Smith). The increase in tension caused by a life strain can also lead to that person becoming particularly vulnerable to further life events. For example, a person who has been experiencing the life strain of severe marital problems will probably be particularly prone to further life events—such as redundancy—causing such an increase in tension level that the stress response and further signs of anxiety are produced.

Having concentrated so far on the physical effects of life events and life strains, the next step is to look at how people may be affected psychologically.

THE PSYCHOLOGICAL EFFECTS OF LIFE EVENTS AND LIFE STRAINS

These effects are very complex, and we can only make a few tentative points at this stage. However, it is likely that life events and life strains affect people psychologically by generally underming (i) their confidence or self-esteem and (ii) their sense of control. (By sense of control we mean the sense of being able to directly influence most of our everyday life.) The two ideas are very closely related.

Looking at the example of redundancy again, it is almost certain that people losing their jobs will suffer a considerable blow to their self-esteem. Their sense of control will also be eroded in such a way that they may eventually feel powerless to do anything about their condition. (As they keep applying for jobs without success, this feeling may be intensified.)

These two effects, decrease in self-esteem and loss of sense of control, are often gradual and, as they cannot be observed, even the person experiencing them may not fully be aware of what is happening. Confidence can drain away imperceptibly under the pressure of life events and life strains. The result of this loss of confidence and loss of feeling of control is that the psychological signs that affect someone will also include a depressed 'hopeless' feeling; he or she will feel helpless, particularly in the face of these seemingly powerful anxiety experiences.

These feelings may partly be due to the nature of the life event or life strain itself. Thus, the breakdown of an important relationship or the loss through death of a loved one will have an obvious impact on our sense of self-esteem, aside from the natural grief at such a loss. We rely on close relationships with relatives or friends to foster our positive feelings about ourselves (this is much more true than many of us realise) so any breakdown in these relationships can lead to significant, if unconscious, effects on our self-esteem.

As well as the effect of the event or strain itself, there is the effect described in the previous section, whereby once a person experiences anxiety attacks, he or she subsequently starts to avoid situations. This, too, will affect a person's self-confidence and sense of control, firstly because they feel they are 'failing' to cope, and secondly by creating a sense of their lives (and even their own bodies) being 'out of control'.

These sorts of feelings may tie in with the person's attitudes, which we discussed in Chapter 2. A person's attitude may cause them to interpret a life event or life strain in such a way as to worsen its effects. For example, a person who had had the early childhood experience of regularly being blamed—punished even—for very trivial things, may well interpret a life event that occurs as an adult (for example a relationship breaking up) as being his or her 'fault', exaggerating the already negative psychological effects of the break-up. Even something that is clearly not the fault of that person, such as redundancy or bereavement, may be interpreted as such through the effect of this sort of attitude.

In the following chapter we will relate these sorts of experiences to the rest of the picture of anxiety we have built up. However, an important point to remember from this chapter is that one of the main factors which allows life events and life strains to have these negative effects is that people are generally quite unaware that these events and strains are affecting them in the ways we have described, notably increasing physical tension, and decreasing self-esteem and sense of control. For this reason, simply by being aware of which life events and life strains may be affecting you, and how and why they are affecting you, you will have taken the first step in learning to deal with them.

SUMMARY

Stressful life events ('**one-off**' experiences such as redundancy) and life strains (**continuous** negative experiences such as significant relationship problems) can be seen as having two closely related kinds of effects on people:

1 Increasing their level of tension
2 Decreasing (i) their self-esteem

(ii) their sense of control

Life events and life strains may work together to create particularly high levels of tension and, likewise, further erode self-confidence. These two effects can occur over long periods of time, and are often outside people's awareness, that is, people are **unconscious** of the effects of life events and life strains. The increase in tension caused by life events and strains makes the triggering of the stress response much more likely, and if this takes place the person will experience an anxiety attack which may seem to come 'out of the blue'. This may lead to avoidance and feelings of helplessness, again damaging self-confidence. Sometimes life events and life strains evoke attitudes which further intensify the negative effects.

However, the most significant fact in this whole process is that people are often unaware that it is taking place. Identifying and understanding the effects of life stresses and life strains is, therefore, a very important part of coping with them.

PROBE QUESTIONNAIRE

1 Write down which significant **life events** you have experienced over the past few years (or in the time before your anxiety problem developed).

2 Write down the **life strains** which are currently affecting you, as well as the ones which affected you at the time your anxiety difficulties started.

3 Write down in detail how these life events and/or life strains probably affected you, in terms of (i) your level of physical tension and (ii) your self-esteem and sense of control. Describe any attitudes you may have, or which you had, which intensified those effects.

The three sides of anxiety, life events and life strains: how they relate together

In previous chapters we have split anxiety into three sides, the physical, the psychological and the behavioural, in order to help our understanding of anxiety. These three sides, of course, are closely related to each other and to the stressful life events and life strains which may cause the anxiety in the first place.

In this chapter we will look at a few ways in which they all affect each other to produce the experience of anxiety.

We have seen in Chapter 5 how life events and life strains can have the following effects on a person:

1 increasing his or her overall level of physical tension
2 decreasing his or her self confidence and sense of control

The first effect, as we have seen, makes the accidental triggering of the stress response (which is easily triggered) much more likely. That person is also particularly vulnerable to the effects of further life events and strains. Even if the full stress response is not triggered, that person's overall anxiety level will increase; they will be in the preparedness state.

The second effect—the loss of confidence—is likely to make a person feel emotionally 'low' or 'nervous', and also make them particularly prone to **negative** thinking (see Chapter 3) which will serve to increase the level of tension still further.

To make this more comprehensible, the above ideas have been set out in diagram form.

If we look at Figure 6.1, the box marked A represents the stressful life events and/or life strains. These lead on to the signs described in box B, namely (i) loss of confidence and (ii) increase in physical tension. This leads in turn to box C, where we see (i) the (possible) accidental triggering of the stress response and (ii) due to a lack of understanding of what is happening, negative thinking about the signs the

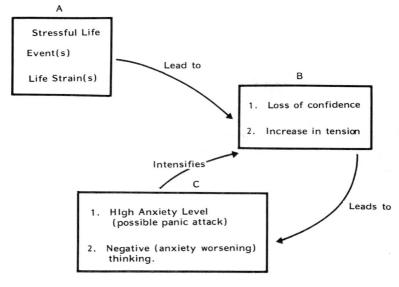

Fig. 6.1

person is experiencing.

There is also a line going back from box C to box B as the signs in box C make the tension and loss of confidence (box B) even worse. In other words, this represents a minor vicious circle: loss of confidence and increase in physical tension lead to either triggering of the stress response or the preparedness state (both creating strong physical signs of anxiety) and negative thinking (for example, 'Am I going crazy?'). This serves to further decrease self-confidence and increase physical tension and so on.

As this vicious circle carries on, a person is likely to avoid situations in which the anxiety signs are particularly bad (and often these are social situations). We can see this in Figure 6.2 in box D, **Behavioural response**. There are two arrows leading from box D. One goes back to box B. This follows the ideas discussed in Chapter 4 on the effects on avoidance. One of these effects is that once you start avoiding situations you start to feel negatively about yourself, so you further undermine your selfconfidence. Secondly, you may find that once you avoid one situation, you then start feeling anxious in other related situations, so your level of tension further

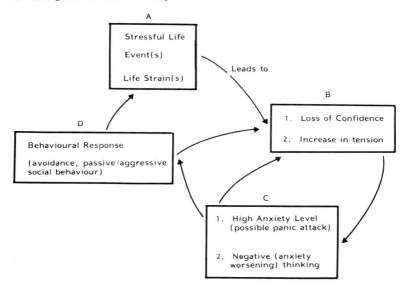

Fig. 6.2

increases. In other words, when you start avoiding situations, anxiety is worsened, and you are more likely to avoid other situations. This is true of the passive behavioural styles described in Chapter 4: when a person fails to act assertively in situations it becomes more difficult to break out of this pattern. In Figure 6.2 you can see that the lines between boxes B, C and D form another vicious circle.

The second line leads from box D to box A. This suggests that once you start avoiding situations, this can lead to further life strains or stresses. For example, a man who has started to avoid social situations, including perhaps going to work, will find this puts additional strain on his family relationships, particularly with his wife. As this carries on, the marital problem itself becomes a further source of stress, affecting self confidence and increasing tension further; the overall vicious circle is complete.

These diagrams are, of course, very simplified; no pictures can do justice to the complexity of a person's experience of anxiety. However, they do point to some of the general features that are usually involved in the signs of anxiety being caused and maintained.

To summarise, the main features to remember are:

1 Life stress or strain may lead to tension and loss of confidence (often a person is not directly aware of this).

2 This can lead to the person being more vulnerable to experiencing the strong physical and psychological signs of anxiety described in Chapters 2 and 3, particularly if the full stress response is triggered.

3 That person's experiences may well seem to come 'out of the blue' and the fear they cause will lead to increased anxiety and loss of confidence.

4 The person may well then start avoiding situations, which will erode self-confidence still further and may lead to tension being experienced in other situations. Also, a person may develop passive (or aggressive) ways of behaving towards others which can further increase tension and reduce confidence.

5 If this carries on, that person may experience further life strains brought on by the avoidance, and the vicious circle is complete.

Your experience of anxiety may be different in many ways, but in order to help you prepare for the second part of this book, try to work out for yourself (in the approximate form of the diagrams shown) just what the pattern of tension or anxiety is in your case. This won't be easy, so you may find it useful just to sit with a paper and a pencil working out different possibilities. Once you find one that is satisfactory, which seems to describe your experience, write it down.

Part two

Coping with stress and anxiety

If you have an anxiety problem, and have read the first part of this book, you should now have a good idea of what anxiety is and why it has come to affect you. As suggested in the beginning of the book, this in itself is a major step in coping with anxiety.
There are still skills which you can learn in anxiety management. These are:

1 Learning the skill of relaxation (which also involves physical fitness).
2 Learning to identify and modify thoughts and attitudes which affect anxiety.
3 Learning to use these skills in **facing** situations.

You will notice that each of these three lines of attack correspond to each of the three sides of anxiety: relaxation training will reduce some of the unnecessary physical reactions; learning to identify and modify thoughts and attitudes will affect the psychological signs of anxiety; behavioural practice will reduce behavioural signs of anxiety.

At the end of each chapter there is a 'target sheet'. You should use this to write out your own plan worked out from that chapter. Each target sheet refers back to the corresponding probe questionnaire in Part One. For example, your replies to the probe questionnaire at the end of Chapter 3 on the psychological side will have pointed out some of the negative thoughts and attitudes which probably affect your anxiety level. In Chapter 8 we look at practical ways of altering thoughts and patterns of thinking, and in the target sheet at the end you can use the information from the probe questionnaire to work out **alternative**, positive and anxiety-reducing thoughts and attitudes.

In Chapter 10 we look at the need to be aware of the life events and strains which may be affecting you, and discuss how the effects of life events and strains can be minimised.

In Chapter 11 suggestions are made about putting all this information together into a complete self-help programme, the main emphasis being on learning and using **practical skills** to overcome anxiety.

Chapter 12 looks at the problems associated with tranquillisers, and ways of dealing with these problems.

Finally, Chapter 13 is a summary of some of the main points covered in this book. You may find it useful to copy this page out and refer to it in situations where you are experiencing anxiety, just to remind yourself of some of the main points.

7 Relaxation training and physical exercise

RELAXATION TRAINING

The idea of relaxation training is not new. It has been recognised for many years that it is very important for each individual to be able to relax. However, it is only in the last twenty years or so that scientists, psychologists in particular, have studied the concept of relaxation closely. It used to be thought that relaxation was something that happened when you were not doing anything; somehow your body just switched off. That is now known to be untrue; for many of us relaxation is a state of body and mind that has to be actively **worked** at; it is in fact a true **skill** and, like any skill, it requires time and effort to learn.

Before looking at the technique of relaxation, we will look at what happens to the mind and body when a person is very relaxed:

1 Heart rate is slow and regular; blood pressure is reduced
2 Respiration (breathing rate) is slow and regular
3 Muscle tension is reduced
4 Psychologically, the person feels calm and relaxed (but not drowsy)
5 Generally the body feels 'quiet', as though it were ticking over quietly and efficiently

You can think of the body as like a car engine in some respects: if a car is well tuned it works more efficiently and uses less petrol; likewise, somebody who regularly allows themselves to become very relaxed is improving the overall efficiency of the body. Someone who is continuously tense is rather like a car which is always being revved too highly, even when it is stationary! Just as that engine will become clogged and inefficient, so will that person feel tense and drained. (It is important to note here that you can be sitting down 'doing nothing' and still be tense. If all your muscles are tensed up you will still be burning up energy excessively and inefficiently, just like the stationary car being revved up. This is why people can feel drained and exhausted at the end of the day, despite believing that they've not actually done anything all day.)

Many people are very tense much of the time—far more tense than is necessary—and rarely get deeply relaxed.

If you look at the pattern of tension for an imaginary man in Figure 7.1, there are two things to notice:

1 He rarely becomes extremely anxious (in other words, he never goes above 75% tension level)
2 He never becomes deeply relaxed

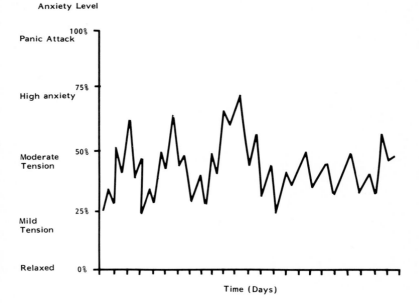

Fig. 7.1

Thus, although he may not have any specific anxiety problems, there are several problems with this consistent level of tension. Firstly, he is likely to experience quite a few of the more vague signs of stress which follow from a moderately high tension level. The following are a few examples: insomnia, regular headaches, feeling tired and listless, never feeling completely calm, stomach ulcers, loss of interest in things (including sex), and irritability.

C

(Although these problems can be caused by other things, they are particularly likely to be associated with high levels of tension.) Secondly, he is more likely to be adversely affected by further pressures, life events and life strains in particular. This is because his tension level is sufficiently high to make further increases in tension serious, leading to significant increases in the various signs of anxiety, including the triggering of the stress response. In this sense he is vulnerable to further stress.

If we look at the tension level of another person, in this case a woman, we can see an example of a different pattern. In Figure 7.2 there are also two things to notice:

1 Her anxiety level (like the man's) never rises above 75%

2 She regularly becomes very deeply relaxed

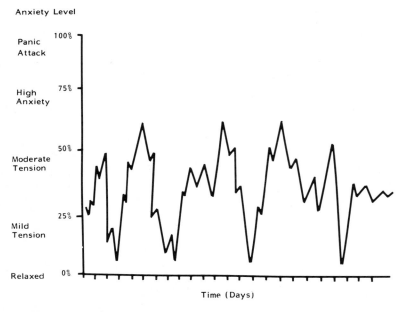

Fig. 7.2

This person will not only be able to cope with stresses and strains far more effectively than the man described above, she will also enjoy a better quality of life. She is able to 'switch off' from all the various day-to-day tensions and consequently feels better in herself. If we return to our example of the car engine, each time you become deeply relaxed, it is as though the engine of your body is being thoroughly serviced and retuned, so that you not only feel better physically and mentally, but you are able to 'go on the road' again and face the regular stresses of everyday life.

PROGRESSIVE DEEP MUSCLE RELAXATION TRAINING

The above title is the full name for a system of exercises developed to help people achieve deep relaxation. The basic concept of these exercises is that by going through each **group** of muscles of the body, alternately tensing then relaxing them, you can eventually do two things:

1 Learn to **identify** tension in the muscles of your body
2 Learn to **reduce** the tension in those muscles

The exercises are written out in detail in the Appendix. They look deceptively simple. In fact, they take considerable time to learn properly. People learning relaxation need to concentrate on the feelings of tension and the feelings of relaxation throughout their bodies as they go through the exercises. Once you have the knack of relaxation, you find that at the end of the exercises the muscles throughout your body feel very relaxed and free from tension.

The reason that **muscle** relaxation is so important is that once you have relaxed all the muscles of the body, the other physical signs of tension we discussed in Chapter 2 are reduced as well, that is, heart rate and blood pressure are reduced, respiration becomes slow and gentle and you feel mentally calm.

Thus, muscular relaxation is the key to general physical and mental relaxation.

CARRYING OUT RELAXATION EXERCISES

The first thing to do is set aside a regular time each day or night to do the exercises. Use a quiet room with a comfortable chair or a bed, and make sure no-one will disturb you. You should then follow the instructions outlined in the Appendix. You can either memorise them or perhaps record them onto tape and simply follow the instructions. (There are a few commercially available relaxation training tapes which are adequate for this.) Whichever method you use, you should give yourself a few weeks of **regular** practice before you judge whether you can do it—you will almost certainly find it very hard at first. You can make relaxing easier by doing the following:

1 Use physical exercise before relaxation (this is described in detail later in this chapter)
2 Have a hot bath before relaxation to help to prepare yourself.
3 Make sure the room you relax in is warm and peaceful.
4 Work out regular, specific times to do the relaxation exercises. Do not leave it to when you feel like it.
5 You may find it useful to combine relaxation with additional related skills, like meditation and yoga. There are often classes which teach these skills which many people find helpful to strengthen their ability to relax and maintain their motivation.
6 Relaxation can be greatly helped by being coupled with massage. Massage is particularly helpful for people who find it hard to relax, as this kind of direct muscular manipulation can be the best way of relieving muscle tension. Going to a trained masseur is the best way to do this, but in the reading list at the end of this book there are a few books which are useful for learning some of the techniques of massage.

Overall, remember that although 'relaxation' sounds simple, it is a genuine skill which takes time and effort to learn. Like any skill it is difficult initially, but becomes easier following regular practice. The benefits can be enormous.

PHYSICAL EXERCISE

In learning to cope with stress and anxiety, physical exercise is an important and often underestimated part of a self-help programme. Physical exercise is important for related reasons. Firstly, as a general rule, the more physically fit a person is, the more that person will be able to cope with stress. To take an example, if you are feeling under the weather, say with a cold or flu, you are more likely to find yourself over-reacting to stresses which you would cope with if you were feeling well. Similarly, if you are generally unfit, you are in a sense in a continual state of being 'under the weather', and are more prone to stress than necessary.

The second reason why exercise is important is rather more technical, and concerns the stress response discussed in Chapter 2. One of the things that happens when the stress response is switched on is that, along with various hormones such as adrenaline, **fatty acids** are released into the bloodstream. These fatty acids are substances that will give extra energy to the muscles and help the 'fight or flight' response. The problem is that, as discussed before, most of the time we do not need to 'fight or flee', so we don't need to use a great deal of muscular effort. These fatty acids and hormones, then, are left in the bloodstream and take time to be used up, and until then do not do us any good. We are left feeling tense and generally 'drained' without being pleasantly tired or relaxed. Physical exercise is, therefore, an excellent way to 'burn up' those fatty acids in the bloodstream. It is one of the best and most natural ways to expend the muscular energy which the stress response has made necessary.

The third reason is related to the two reasons above, and concerns relaxation training. Relaxation training is a skill which takes time and practice to acquire, so it is important to make it as easy as possible. If you try to relax when you are feeling tense you will find it more difficult than if you are already feeling quite relaxed. If you do your relaxation training exercises after having done some physical exercise, you will find that you feel more physically prepared to relax, having 'burned off' the excess tension through the exercise.

The fourth reason is that people who regularly exercise are likely to feel more positive about themselves; in other words, exercise can lead to a general sense of physical well-being. This can be very significant if we consider that one of the problems with anxiety is that a person feels 'out of control' of his or her own body.

For these reasons it is important, especially if you do not currently do much exercise, to work out a programme of exercise to improve your physical health. **However, it is very important to check with your G.P. to make sure there are no physical reasons why you should not undertake an exercise programme.**

WHAT SORT OF EXERCISE?

Most exercises are a combination of two ways of improving the functioning of the body. The first way of improving fitness is to increase the strength or tone of all the various muscle groups. The second way is to improve the efficiency of the heart and lung system. Although all exercises are a combination of the two, different exercise usually emphasise one sort of improvement over the other. For example, weight training and various gym exercises primarily increase muscular strength. Other exercises, like jogging and running, will primarily improve heart/lung efficiency, but also tone up leg muscles (but will do little to improve the tone of, for example, chest/arm muscles). Perhaps the best solution is to try a combination of the two: one sort of exercise which primarily helps improve heart/lung efficiency, and one which builds muscular tone.

One of the best exercises of all is regular swimming. It is ideal because once you have learned to swim, and got used to different strokes, it is an excellent way of improving heart/lung efficiency, and, at the same time, exercises most muscle groups very effectively without straining them.

In terms of general exercise there are a number of books which describe different sorts of physical exercise, and the reference list at the end of the book suggests one of the most straightforward (and least expensive!).

Whichever programme you work out for yourself, the most important thing to remember is that you should start with very brief, gentle exercise and only very gradually build the level up as your fitness improves. The first step should be to check with your G.P.

TARGET SHEET

1 **Relaxation Training.** Work out a timetable specifying when you can follow the relaxation training exercises. Try to do them daily, particularly at first, and leave yourself at least 40 minutes. Also, decide the best way you should do relaxation. Are you going to memorise the instructions, make a tape or have someone read them to you? Decide now and write out your time-

table on a piece of paper.

2 **Physical Exercise.** Having checked with your G.P. first, and then bought necessary equipment/books, work out a timetable for the **exercise** you will be doing. Stick to this timetable once you have decided it, and try to make both exercise and relaxation a regular part of your life from now on.

$\mathscr{8}$ Psychological methods

In Chapter 3 we looked at the three different areas of the psychological side of anxiety:

1 The specific anxiety-provoking things you think or say to yourself
2 The actual **feelings** of fear
3 The attitudes you have to people or situations which may bring on or worsen anxiety.

In this chapter we will look at psychological methods of dealing with these three areas, and it is particularly important to refer back to the probe questionnaire you did at the end of Chapter 3. We will take each of the three areas of the psychological side of anxiety in turn.

ADAPTING ANXIETY-PROVOKING THOUGHTS

When a person experiences anxiety, how he or she **thinks** about that anxiety will greatly affect how the anxiety develops. As we saw in Chapter 3 most people who experience the physical signs (palpitations; etc.) will also feel nervous or fearful. They will then tend to think certain things, or label their feelings in very negative ways (e.g. 'I'm going to go off my head'). If you answered the probe questionnaire at the end of Chapter 3 you will have identified a number of these thoughts or ideas that affect you. It is very important to work at replacing these sorts of thoughts with ones which will significantly decrease anxiety, rather than worsen it. The following list contains a number of examples of positive ideas and self-statements which people have found useful:

1 These feelings will not harm me, I just need to relax
2 I just have to let go of the tension, there is no need to fight it
3 As I relax myself, so all the feelings of anxiety will

ease off

4 There is no need to escape or avoid situations, if I just carry on the anxiety will subside
5 Just 'flow with the anxiety'
6 I can cope with these feelings
7 Relax, breathe gently, let the tension go
8 Anxiety is not harmful, it is a normal human response

These simple-sounding ideas relate to all the information on anxiety you have absorbed through reading this book. If someone tried to use them without reading the first part of the book they would not be anywhere near as effective. If you look back to Chapter 3 and the section on anxiety-provoking thoughts, you will recall that these thoughts bring to the surface of the mind other negative ideas and memories of which the person may be unaware but which nevertheless affect that person's mood. The list above, on the other hand, will bring to mind all the positive things you have learned about anxiety, for example that it is normal, that it will not harm you, that it has nothing to do with losing your mind and so on, and this information will positively affect your mood.

It is also important to work out alternatives to the 'automatic' negative thoughts, the ones which are so habitual that you may not have noticed their existence. Automatic semi-conscious ideas like 'I'm not going to be able to cope' need to be replaced with their positive counterparts.

Generally, negative thinking can become a very ingrained, often unnoticed habit, so it is very important to identify and adapt negative thoughts. This will seem artificial at first, but as you practice the positive, alternative thoughts two things happen:

1 These new thoughts actually work in helping you cope with anxiety
2 They gradually become more 'natural' as you get used to them; you are basically replacing one (negative) habit with another (positive) one, and of course changing habits involves hard work, especially at first

At the end of this chapter on the target sheet you will be asked to refer back to your responses to the probe questionnaire in Chapter 3 where you recorded the particular things you think when anxious which worsen the anxiety. Using the list of positive statements above as a guide, you should go through your old responses and adjust them so that they are positive and accurate. Think particularly about information in the book you have found especially helpful, or which has struck you as relevant to **your** difficulties, and then **use** this information as a basis for constructing new, positive self-statements.

Remember that negative thinking can become a very ingrained, almost unnoticed habit, so it is very important to identify and adapt these sorts of 'automatic' negative thoughts, such as 'I just can't cope'.

COPING WITH THE FEELINGS OF FEAR AND NERVOUSNESS

As we saw in Chapter 3, the feelings of fear and nervousness are the emotional aspect of the stress response and preparedness state. These emotional feelings help motivate us to do something about physical threat or a stress (e.g. an examination) we have to face. The problem is that when we feel nervous or frightened when there is no obvious external reason, we tend to label the feelings very negatively. This is closely tied in with the points made about anxiety-provoking thoughts: by replacing the negative **labels** you may attach to feelings of fear ('I must be going mad') with a positive, accurate label ('I may be tense but it's not going to harm me; just relax') you will significantly affect the feeling of fear itself. Remember, the increased emotionality, particularly the feeling of fear, is very much part of the normal bodily reaction to stress.

A second way of dealing with feelings of fear relies on developing the skill of relaxation training and using it in real life situations. As you become better at relaxing and 'letting go' you will find that the bodily reaction to stress is increasingly reduced. Relaxation becomes an alternative to emotionality the more you practice it. Obviously, in many stressful situations we can never totally relax, but even in these situations (such as facing a difficult interview) the stronger our ability to relax, the less intense the feelings of nervousness will be.

ADAPTING ATTITUDES WHICH CREATE ANXIETY

This is the most difficult area since, as we saw in Chapter 3, people are:

1 Often not directly aware of their attitudes
2 Attitudes are often formed early on in life and so tend to be deeply rooted

There are many examples of attitudes which are related to the experience of anxiety, and we saw several of these in the section on attitudes in Chapter 3.

The principle underlying this section on changing these sorts of attitudes is this:

> Once you become aware of a negative (anxiety-inducing) attitude it leads to, you work at changing the behaviour rather than the attitude itself. This will lead to attitudes being changed.

This is the opposite way around to the way most people see attitude change and they might say this: 'If you have a negative attitude, change this, and then your behaviour will change.'

In fact a lot of psychological research has not confirmed this second view; it appears to be far more effective if we 'leapfrog' the attitude, and aim at directly changing the behaviour related to the attitude. This leads to new **experiences** which then modify the underlying attitude.

We will look at the case of Susan Brown which was described on page 25. Re-read this case to remind yourself of the details. In this case Susan's attitude to herself was very negative, she was rarely if ever assertive with other people and constantly avoided social contact because of the anxiety it caused her:

With her family, if ever she felt they were treating her negatively, she said nothing, but if things carried on and became too bad she would eventually get so upset that she would shout and cry at them, and feel foolish and guilty afterwards. Having expressed her upset in this way she would then go back to her previous behaviour. We have identified her negative attitudes about herself. The behaviour associated with this attitude (which we looked at in Chapter 4) comprised **avoidance** of social situations and a passive (as opposed to assertive) way of relating to people. Susan worked out this outline of her behaviour, and then filled in this outline with more detail, looking at specific situations she has been in where she had been passive. This enabled her to work out alternative ways of dealing with situations.

Susan was fortunate in that she had a very close friend whom she trusted, and she was able to discuss this with her. Her friend who was more self-confident, helped her by acting out some situations. She chose a few key situations which caused her difficulties, one example being to deal with her older brother, who often teased her and made her feel bad, although she never told him this. She also decided to work on her avoidance of social situations by enrolling for evening classes. Susan worked at identifying the negative thinking she had nearly always employed previously, and she spent some time looking at the actual behaviour she needed to change. For example, rather than hiding in the corner and not saying anything, she decided that evening classes would give her a chance to actually start conversations with other people. All these changes were, of course, frightening to her. Once she 'took the plunge' and started trying to change her behaviour in this way, despite hiccups she gradually found her view of herself changing; she no longer felt so negative about herself, and her anxiety in a number of situations diminished significantly.

This case illustrates how behaviour change often needs to come **before** attitude change can occur, although the very first thing that had to happen was that Susan decided that she **wanted** to change.

This area of attitude change overlaps with the following chapter on behavioural targets, and more examples will be discussed there.

Another sort of anxiety-creating attitude which we looked at in Chapter 3 was the widespread attitude that it is somehow 'weak' for men to display vulnerability in front of others. This can lead to vulnerability and self-doubt being suppressed, and false 'fronts' developing instead. This can produce a marked tension between real feelings and the unreal 'front'. We all experience having to 'act confidently', and at times it is probably necessary. We also saw above how Susan Brown learned to feel more confident by behaving as though she were! The difficulty lies in the pressure to constantly adopt a position of invulnerability. There is an enormous pressure in this society for men to conform to this position; from the earliest days boys learn that it is 'sissy' to be upset, for example.

The attitudes that are produced by this pressure cannot be changed overnight, of course, but it is important for the individual to recognise their effects.

Men who experience anxiety sometimes find that the inability to even recognise, let alone express, feelings of self-doubt is connected with their experience of anxiety. For them it is important to recognise this attitude and to work at expressing these feelings. Often the result is that they find these feelings are shared, and that they are a natural (and desirable) part of being human.

Paul Daines had been married for several years. He had not had much sexual experience before he was married, nor had his wife. Although their sex life had started off all right, it soon became fraught with difficulties. He wasn't sure if his wife enjoyed their love-making and he found it impossible to ask her about her feelings. He felt he should know all about sex and listening to his men friends, it seemed as if he were the only one having any difficulties. He felt inadequate, and was not able to voice these feelings to anybody. As a result, the love-making between Paul and his wife deteriorated to the point where they rarely made love. This created a great strain within their relationship, with the eventual result that both started to experience signs of stress.

This example illustrates how Paul's inability to discuss his sexual relationship with his wife led to the difficulties continuing unresolved. He felt very strongly that men should 'know' automatically what sex is all about, and his friends, films, and T.V. all seemed to confirm this. For Paul the first step was to recognise that this is not the case. He had to learn to share his feelings of inadequacy with his wife, to see these feelings as being natural, and discover that his wife had similar feelings as well. He came to see that hiding vulnerability is the problem, not vulnerability itself.

We have only looked at two examples of the sorts of anxiety-inducing attitudes that affect people. Other attitudes which can affect people involve the following sorts of beliefs:

1 I must be successful at everything I do; failure is unforgivable

2 I must always put other people's needs before my own. I have no right to do things for myself

3 I am basically useless, there is no real point in trying to change anything

These are basic beliefs some people have about themselves. They probably do not say these things to themselves, but if we look at their attitudes and behaviour, it is often the case that deep down that is the belief behind everything. For these sorts of beliefs, the best approach is that outlined in the examples of Susan and Paul: identify the belief and attitudes; look at the behaviour this leads to; make a plan of action to change the behaviour; follow this through **consistently** and the belief and attitudes can eventually change in line with the behaviour.

In your replies to the questionnaire at the end of Chapter 3, you should have noted down one or two attitudes which you may feel help to bring on or worsen the anxiety which you experience. In the following target sheet note these down and work out the basic beliefs which may be behind them, and the behaviour that they lead to. After reading the next chapter come back to this and work out a practical plan to change your behaviour in selected situations, starting off with simple situations and building up to more difficult ones. Couple this with the changes you need to make in the other two areas of the psychological side of anxiety, concerning the specific thoughts and emotions you have. These three areas are closely related and it is important to link the three together in your self-help plan.

TARGET SHEET

1 **Anxiety-provoking thoughts.** Check back to your replies to the questionnaire at the end of Chapter 3 concerning the specific things you think to yourself which bring on, or worsen, the signs of anxiety you experience. Using the set of **positive** statements in this chapter as a guide, work out a set of statements for yourself to use in anxiety-provoking situations.

2 **Label emotional feelings** positively and correctly in the same way.

3 **Anxiety-provoking attitudes.** Again check back to your replies to the questionnaire at the end of Chapter 3 concerning the attitudes you may have which serve to bring on or worsen anxiety. On a separate sheet, spend as much time as necessary looking at the basic belief(s) which may be behind the attitude(s); try to sum it up in a single statement as in the examples given in this chapter. Next, work out the behaviour this belief and attitude leads to. Just jot down what you actually **do** in various situations. Read the following chapter on behavioural practice, then return to this list. Add to it if necessary, and then construct a list of **alternative** things you should do in these situations. Spend some time on this list; we will return to it in Chapter 11.

⑨ Behavioural targets

OVERCOMING AVOIDANCE

For many people with an anxiety problem, avoidance, as we discussed in Chapter 4, is one of the main ways that their lives are affected practically. This is particularly the case when people avoid **social** situations, as inevitably the quality of life is considerably worsened.

The reasons why people initially start to avoid situations has already been discussed, so the focus of this chapter is how people can set about reversing this process.

The first thing to be said is that to overcome avoidance, you will need to face up to situations, to confront the fear itself. People never overcome avoidance without having experienced extra anxiety for a while. The question is how to do this in a way which does not involve excessive amounts of anxiety, and which is also very effective, so we will now look at one of the most useful methods of doing this.

GRADED PRACTICE

Graded practice is a method in which a person who is particularly anxious in certain situations, for example social situations, works out a hierarchy of situations, from ones which only cause that person a small amount of tension, all the way up to those situations which create the maximum amount of anxiety.

For example, Audrey Wilkinson suffered from an anxiety problem which is often described as agoraphobia: she would experience all the various signs of anxiety whenever she was away from the 'safety' of her home, particularly in crowded social situations. She worked out a 'fear hierarchy' starting off with easy situations and working up to ones which were very difficult for her to face, and which she always avoided:

1 Going to the end of her front garden and standing for

a moment when the street is very quiet
2 Going for a short walk down the street and back when it is quiet
3 Going to the end of her front garden and standing for a moment when the street is quite busy
4 Walking down her street when it is busy
5 Going to the corner shop when it is empty
6 Catching a bus with a friend when it is very quiet
7 Going to the corner shop when it has a few people there
8 Catching a busy bus with a friend
9 Going to the supermarket with a friend
10 Catching a busy bus alone
11 Going to the local pub with her husband
12 Going to the supermarket alone

With **graded practice** the goal for Audrey was to gradually work through the list of situations, starting off with the easy ones, practising each in turn until she became confident enough to go on to the next one.

Whilst practising these situations she also, of course, used the techniques discussed in Chapters 7 and 8, that is, making sure that she relaxed as far as possible and she approached the situations in the right frame of mind.

However, she never felt **fully** confident about taking on the next situation in the hierarchy, so with each new situation she had to use her courage and 'plunge in'. This is a very important point which is worth discussing further.

If you experience anxiety symptoms in various situations, you will need to **practise** **using** these skills in different situations. You will probably not feel very confident **before** you enter each situation, it is only **after** you have been in the situation that you will feel confident about facing it! If you think about it, this is true of our confidence about trying out all new situations. An obvious example is learning to drive a car. You could read all the books there are about driving, and they would only give you a little bit of confidence about what to actually do. To gain the real confidence you have to sit behind the wheel and actually experience **doing** it. As you start to experience the reality of driving a car, you then start to use the information you acquired through reading the books.

In terms of anxiety, when you put yourself in a situation which you have been avoiding for a long time, or perhaps a situation you have never faced, you will be in the same situation as the person behind the wheel of a car for the first time; through reading this book you will know what the anxiety is, and you will know in theory how to deal with it. The task now is to actually **practise it in real life**. Just as learning to drive takes practise, so learning to cope with and control anxiety takes practise as well.

In the example of Audrey Wilkinson, the graded practise procedure helped her recover her confidence by gradually 'taking on' new situations. Looking at our example of driving, it was the equivalent of having the first lesson in a quiet cul-de-sac, and gradually starting to go on to busier roads. Remember, confidence comes **after** you have faced up to the situation, not before.

Audrey's problem was agoraphobia. The principle of graded practise is relevant for all sorts of difficulties where avoidance is concerned, from fear of spiders to fear of heights and so on. In each case it is possible to work out this hierarchy of situations, and then to work through it, step by step, confronting the fear in a graded fashion until avoidance is overcome.

At the end of the chapter you will find the target sheet with which you can construct your own hierarchy for those situations you currently avoid. In Chapter 11 ('Putting it all together') we will look at how your hierarchy (or hierarchies) can be linked with other aspects of your self-help plan.

ALTERING SOCIAL BEHAVIOUR

In Chapter 4 we saw how the ways people behave **socially** can be connected with the experience of anxiety, and a useful way of looking at social behaviour involves the ideas of:

1 Assertiveness
2 Passivity
3 Aggression

If you look at your own behaviour carefully, you may find that you may be approaching situations with attitudes which produce either aggressive, passive or assertive behaviour.

We'll take an example to illustrate this further.

Louise Davis is an office worker. She tends to feel anxious in situations such as when she goes out with people in her office for a drink at lunch times, or other social occasions. She doesn't like it when the men make vaguely sexual suggestions to her, as these make her feel tense and embarrassed and sometimes angry. However, she doesn't usually say anything. Her attitude is that they don't mean any harm, so she shouldn't make a fuss; there might be a scene if she did. She finds these situations very difficult though, and always feels angry with herself afterwards for not saying anything.

This is a very simple example, but it does illustrate how Louise's attitude to this situation led to her behave rather passively, and this in turn led to her feeling negative about herself and anxious about the situation. Finally, of course, it meant that her male colleagues' behaviour continued.

Perhaps the most significant part of this example is that she felt there might be a scene if she spoke up. People who tend to be passive often find it hard to distinguish between assertive or aggressive behaviour. An aggressive response in this situation, slapping the man across the face for example, would be likely to create a scene. (The man may deserve a slap but the negative consequences for Louise may cause more, not less, problems.) Politely telling the man that she would rather he did not make such remarks to her and explaining why is less likely to cause a scene, and may perhaps lead to his behaviour eventually improving. Even if it didn't, the fact that she has stood up for herself makes it worthwhile in terms of her feelings about herself. The general point, as we saw in the last chapter, is that by being aware of attitudes which lead to passive behaviour, you can then work at changing the behaviour itself. Once you regularly respond assertively, you find the passive attitude changes. In Louise's example, by continually responding to the derogatory sexist remarks of her colleagues in an assertive manner, she found her attitude to these sort of situations changed. Rather than the attitude: 'They mean no harm, I'll only cause a scene if I say anything' she felt instead: 'What they are doing is offensive even if they are unaware of it; it's up to me to stand up for myself to them'.

In this case Louise also found it useful to start learning self-defence, as it helped her feel more positive about her physical ability to stand up for herself, making assertive behaviour much easier. Developing assertive behaviour like this is, however, difficult, especially at first when being assertive can seem quite risky and you feel very nervous about the possible consequences. But generally being assertive does have a positive pay-off in terms of self-image; you will feel better about yourself for having stood up for your rights.

Similarly, some people develop an aggressive style of relating to people and this, too, can lead to personal difficulties.

Jeff Howard came from a background in which he had to be tough and independent to get what he wanted. As he grew older he still kept this attitude, and although it helped him achieve success at work (he was in business) he found it did not lead to success in relationships. He related to his friends in an aggressive, competitive way, usually involving sporting activities such as squash. He felt that the only alternative to being aggressive was being feeble, so he despised anyone else who was not as aggressive as himself. Predictably, he had particular problems in seeing women as equals and his behaviour towards them ultimately resulted in relationships collapsing in one way or another. Although he was successful in money terms, he was aware of there being a huge gap in his life, which of course there was.

For Jeff the problem was that he had to learn that aggressive behaviour is not a measure of strength, rather it is a measure of lack of imagination. He needed to try out different ways of relating to people, in particular learning to put his own needs second.

This was for him a difficult plan, as he had to constantly monitor his own reaction to situations and try to avoid his usual responses. This was particularly the case with people who were not aggressive like him, and he had to work very hard to see things from their point of view.

There are many examples of aggressive, passive and assertive social behaviour, and every single person shows elements of each one every day. However, if you can identify a tendency to be 'locked' into one particular way of relating to people, it is important to develop positive alternatives. For a lot of people this is likely to be a long-term plan, so it will be important to link this aspect of social behaviour with the other aspects of a self-help plan, and perhaps the section on attitude change is particularly relevant in this.

Use the target sheet to generate a number of practical steps to overcoming both avoidance and/or passivity/aggression.

TARGET SHEET

Look back to your replies to the probe questionnaire at the end of Chapter 4.

1 If there are situations which you are totally avoiding, on a separate page work out a **graded practice** hierarchy starting from those situations which produce fairly mild anxiety, through those which at present would produce the greatest anxiety. Try to arrange the hierarchy so there are quite a few small steps (ten or so) rather than just two or three big steps. There may also be situations which you are 'half avoiding'. For example, you may only face up to some situations if you are accompanied. You can still write out a hierarchy for these situations using the same principle. Start with what you are doing currently, and work out increasingly difficult steps until the final item includes confronting the situation unassisted.

2 Identify ways you respond to other people which are predominantly passive or aggressive. Look at specific examples if possible, and then generate alternative **assertive** behavioural responses. Write out some situations (using the graded practice method if possible) where you can practise and develop assertive behaviour.

10 Coping with stressful life events and life strains

There are many different life events and life strains which may affect people, and each person reacts to them differently from others. Not enough is known either about life events and strains or about people themselves to specify how people cope with the life events in any detail.

However, there are a few general ideas which the reader may find useful in helping to minimise the negative effects of life events and strains. Perhaps the most important thing is to **recognise** an event or a strain. As we saw in Chapter 5 people are often **unaware** of the general increase in physical tension and loss of confidence that is caused by strain, such as continuing domestic problems or work difficulties. People may also be unaware of the fact that after a 'one off' life event, such as an accident, they may be more tense (and therefore more vulnerable to the effects of further stress or strain) for some time afterwards. When people are unaware of these effects, then they are unlikely to do anything about the stress or strain causing them.

Therefore, it is very important that you **recognise** and **separate** the various pressures that may be affecting you. Some of them you may not be able to do much about, but having recognised them you can at least (i) understand them and (ii) work at changing your **reactions** to them. You may at this point find it necessary to go back to the questionnaire at the end of Chapter 5 and spend some more time working out what life events have affected you and what life strains are currently affecting you.

Having listed these strains, there will probably be some that you can actually work at **changing** directly. For example, if one of the strains you have identified is that your marriage has become humdrum, so you are bored and dissatisfied, then there are probably a number of practical things you could do with your husband or wife to set about getting out of this rut.

In this example discussing the problem with your spouse

is the first step before looking at ways of dealing with it; many couples get into a rut this way with both partners feeling vaguely dissatisfied without summoning the courage to voice their feelings. It is by voicing a dissatisfaction that you can start to look at ways of dealing with it.

A method which you may find useful in helping you work out some of the strains you are experiencing is known as the problem-solving technique, outlined in the six stages below:

1 Define the problem as clearly as possible
2 Generate as many solutions as possible and write them down. **Do not be selective**, write down every possibility that occurs to you
3 Having generated this list go through each solution in turn, noting the advantages or disadvantages of each
4 Select which solution (or solutions) is (or are) the most practical
5 Specify how, when and with whom you can put it into practice
6 Do it!

This method may seem fairly obvious, but in fact people often do not work on problems as systematically as this; instead they dwell on them, and often end up feeling negative rather than dealing with the problems effectively. You may find this approach generates quite a few ideas which will help in minimising the effects of some strains, especially those which have previously been vague and ill-defined (but whose negative effects have been significant despite that).

For example, if an identified strain is looking after an elderly frail relative, then the problem-solving technique may generate quite a few ideas to minimise the pressure, such as arranging for other relatives to look after this person at specific regular times, arranging day care for a few days a week and so on. These ideas may well have occurred to the person before, but following the problem-solving procedure helps the person make a concrete and practical plan of action rather than having just a few vague ideas.

It is also useful to use the problem-solving technique with others who are also involved in your difficulties. Friends and relatives can sometimes be enlisted to help generate ideas and can often suggest things you would not think of yourself.

The problem-solving technique can be a very powerful tool, and many people have found it invaluable in giving them ideas for practical approaches to problems. As it is such a flexible tool for a variety of problems, further examples are unlikely to be relevant to your difficulty, so be prepared to tackle this difficulty using the problem-solving technique seriously, and spend some time doing so; it will be easier the more you become acquainted with the approach.

Major life strains such as unemployment are, of course, more resistant to being minimised in the way outlined above but it is still important to try to deal with them as best as possible. For strains like unemployment which can severely affect self-esteem, perhaps the best approach is for the person to concentrate on building up those activities and interests which represent alternative sources of self-esteem. This is not to try to make unemployment somehow more 'acceptable'—it clearly is not—rather, it is to minimise the debilitating personal consequences as far as possible. As work is such an important factor in this respect, it is likely that the person without work will need several **different** sources of reinforcement to maintain their self-esteem; physical fitness, enrolling in evening classes, pursuing hobbies, joining 'self-help' organisations such as the Claimant's Union are amongst the various possibilities which should be looked at.

This last point about joining self-help or support groups is particularly important. There are many such groups for people who have had or are having stressful experiences, and they can perform an important function in helping people form an understanding of the difficulties they face, and sharing experiences about these difficulties. For example, women who have been sexually assaulted will find the support and advice of Rape Crisis Centres useful; people who have suffered bereavement may find the organisation 'Cruse' for widows and widowers a source of help and so on. Contacting your local Citizens Advice Bureau or local Social Services is one way of finding out about such groups where you live.

For other strains, such as that caused by the inherently stressful nature of a person's job, the best approach may be to minimise the physical effects of tension. In Chapter 7 we discussed how important physical exercise can be, so for the person in a high stress job 'burning off' the physical effects of tension by exercise may be a **necessary** and a regular part of their self-help programme.

Finally, all the ideas in this chapter are based on the following general truth: whatever the problem facing a person, it is almost always the case that by **doing something** about that problem, no matter how slight, the person will be reducing the negative impact, including the feeling of helplessness, of that problem. It is this feeling of helplessness which is often the most significant experience following life events and strains. Helplessness results in people simply feeling unable to do anything about their situation. This chapter shows that it is possible to do **something** about stress and strains, and understanding their significance is often the first step in relieving this helplessness which can seriously undermine self-confidence.

To summarise this chapter, as several key issues have been raised: although people's reactions to life events and life strains are highly complex and barely understood, there are a few general ideas which people may find useful in coping with them.

1 Recognising and separating life events and life strains is the first step
2 The technique known as 'problem-solving' can be useful in helping a person work out ideas and make a practical plan to minimise the strain itself
3 Some major strains cannot be directly attacked in this way. However, their negative effects on the person can be minimised by (i) actively **building up** self-esteem through alternative sources and/or (ii) reducing the physical effects of the strain. Self-help organisations exist for many problems, and these can provide invaluable sources of support and understanding
4 Generally **doing something** about strain once it is identified is the important factor in combating the sense of helplessness that follows many life events and strains

TARGET SHEET

Refer back to your replies to the probe questionnaire at the

end of Chapter 5 in which you listed the main life events
and strains which have affected or which are affecting you.

On a separate sheet go through the strains which are
currently affecting you, and use the **problem-solving
technique** to generate possible solutions. Once this is
done write out the coping strategies you have decided
upon in the space below. For those strains or events
which in themselves cannot be dealt with, work out
ways of minimising their effects on you (particularly
tension-reducing techniques like relaxation and physical
exercise) and building up self-esteem through separate
activities. Again write out the coping strategies on a
sheet of paper.

11 Putting it all together in a self-help programme

If you have been following the suggestions in this book closely then you will have written down a number of plans to help you learn to deal with the three different sides of anxiety as well as looking at ways of minimising the effects of life events and life strains. In this chapter we will look at ways of collecting all this information together in a way which maximises the effectiveness of your self-help programme.

If we look at the three sides of anxiety, and the suggested approaches to deal with each side, we can plan it out in a diagram, which also includes stressful life events and life strains.

In Figure 11.1, each of the three sides is given equal weighting, with the stressful life events and strains in the central section. However, for each person the weighting for each side may be very different. For example, a business executive suffering from high stress may not be avoiding any situations, and may not have any major problems with passive or aggressive behaviour in social situations. For her the behavioural side would be very small. Instead, she would concentrate on the two other sides, the psychological side, and the physical side, as well as identifying particular strains in her day-to-day life. The overall 'shape' of her programme would look like that in Figure 11.2.

To summarise her self-help programme very briefly: she would concentrate on the physical side (relaxation and exercise) and the psychological side, where she would work out significant attitudes which led to her spending too much time involved in work, and not enough time looking after her social needs. Related to this she would also identify particular life strains (especially at work) and use the problem-solving technique to generate a number of ideas for using her time at work more efficiently, relieving some of the stress she had been experiencing.

You too should be able to estimate how important each of

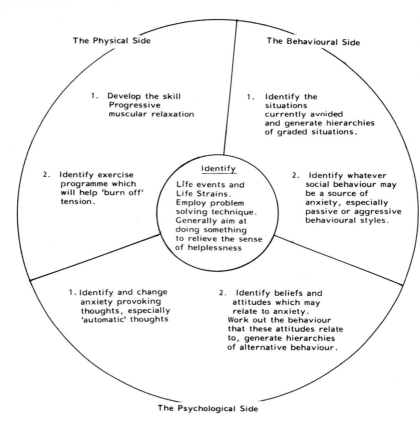

Fig. 11.1

the three sides is in terms of your particular anxiety difficulties, and concentrate the majority of your attention on those that are most significant.

The next step is to decide which side· of the anxiety to start on. Probably most people will find it easiest to start on the physical side, by working out a plan including relaxation training and physical exercise. There are several reasons for starting in this way:

1 The skill of relaxation is used in the other two; for example, being able to relax and 'let go' of the tension are important positive thoughts used to replace negative

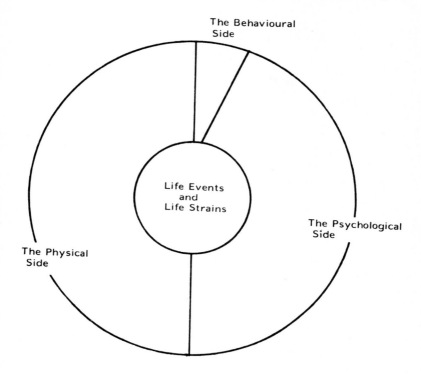

Fig. 11.2

anxiety-producing ones. Also, when you are confronting situations you will find it useful to be able to relax.

2 Relaxation training and physical exercise are probably the most practical of the skills, and you will probably find it helpful to start with the more practical side. Using your target sheet as a basis, work out a specific detailed programme of exercise and relaxation. Set aside specific times on specific days. Write your programme out in detail so you don't have to decide each day what you should do; if you leave it to your mood you will probably not get started. By having a timetable for relaxation exercises you are essentially optimising your motivation and willpower.

The second side to look at is the psychological side. The reason for this is that it is best to prepare yourself psychologically before actually confronting situations (the behavioural side).

The two aspects of the psychological side, replacing anxiety-provoking thoughts with positive, anxiety-reducing ones, and identifying and changing attitudes and beliefs through changing the behaviour associated with them, are both rather more difficult. Start off by concentrating (if you have not already done it) on the first aspect, replacing anxiety-provoking thoughts with positive ones.

At this stage writing these thoughts out might seem rather artificial; it is very important to do so, however, since by working them out and writing them down, you will be preparing yourself to use them in real situations. We discussed in Chapter 10 how it is only once you have actually started using these ideas in practice that your confidence in them will grow.

The second aspect, changing attitudes, is perhaps the most difficult part of a self-help programme. As we mentioned in Chapters 3 and 8, attitudes are hard to define as we are often unaware of them, and they are also often deeply ingrained. Nevertheless, by identifying the negative beliefs and attitudes the first vital step has been made. It is best to see the changing attitudes as a more long-term part of the programme. As we have said, by **consistently** and **regularly** working at changing the behaviour associated with the attitude, you will gradually alter the attitude itself. For example, someone who is excessively competitive can gradually work at taking things easier, discovering that people still respect you if you are not aggressively seeking to be 'on top'. Changing behaviour in this way is not easy, so in your programme work out a graded hierarchy, detailing specific situations, and outlining what you feel the 'improved' behaviour would be. As with changing actual thoughts, initially this seems artificial (as well as hard work) but it will in time be effective as the behaviour change becomes more stable, more 'real' (as in the example of the person for whom the skill of driving becomes real only· after he or she gets behind the wheel of the car and starts driving). The consequences of the behaviour change will deepen; attitudes and beliefs will come gradually into alignment with behaviour.

The behavioural side of anxiety, avoidance in particular, can be started on as soon as you are able to practise relaxation, and also when you have become aware of and altered specific anxiety-producing thoughts. As with relaxation, it is very important to write out in detail a hierarchy of the situations you avoid, and start working through them regularly and consistently. The major point here is that you will probably never feel very confident about facing up to a new situation you have previously avoided. Therefore, if you depend on 'feeling in the mood' before you try it out, you will probably keep putting it off. So again write out a programme, perhaps on a weekly basis, where you specify what situation you will face, where and when. Then start actually **doing** it. Look also at your social behaviour; identify whether aggression or passivity is part of the problem. Someone who is passive (under-assertive) can gradually practise more assertive approaches to (initially simple) situations, and will eventually acquire more confidence. (This area of social behaviour may, of course, closely overlap with the psychological side of anxiety, particularly attitudes.)

Finally, if you have not already done it, define the life events which may have affected you recently and, more importantly, those life strains that affect you now. Work out which ones you can do something about, keeping in mind the main point that events and strains erode self-confidence and increase tension very gradually without a person even noticing. Building confidence and reducing tension are, therefore, vitally important if the strains cannot be attacked directly. If you can do something about the strain, then again work out in a detailed way how you can set about changing it.

As you actually start to follow through the programme you have devised from reading this book, it will start to make real sense to you as your own **experience** starts to change.

As suggested at the beginning of the book, just reading this book without doing anything about it may help people to a certain extent, but the best help is self-help, and once you start carrying out the practical side of the book, then the idea of coping with stress and anxiety will stop being just an idea, and become a reality.

Good luck!

POSTSCRIPT

Although I will not be able to enter into a personal correspendence, I will be very interested in receiving people's comments about this book, positive and negative. I am particularly interested in hearing about people's self-help programmes, and also about other ideas and techniques not mentioned in this book which people have found useful. All information will be treated in strictest confidence. Please write to: Bob Whitmore, c/o Manchester University Press, Oxford Road, Manchester M13 9PL.

12 Tranquillisers and anxiety

Tranquillisers and sleeping pills are the most commonly prescribed drugs in Britain today. Recently there has been concern over the use of tranquillisers for several reasons:

1 They may have unpleasant **side effects**, such as drowsiness, weakness, dry mouth, etc.
2 People are at risk of becoming **dependent** on tranquillisers, that is, they may become psychologically and physically **addicted** to them
3 There is evidence that they are no longer effective after six months' use, but despite this many people carry on taking them for much longer periods
4 People may experience **withdrawal symptoms** (such as increased anxiety, insomnia, trembling, etc.) when they try to cut them down or do without them altogether

Although a short course of tranquillisers may help people over a particularly stressful time, such as following a bereavement or a similar crisis, there is a danger that (i) they carry on being taken long after the crisis is over or (ii) they are prescribed for the effects of general stress (such as that caused by marital problems) rather than tackling the stress itself. People who go to their G.P. complaining of anxiety signs are often unaware of the physical mechanism which causes the signs (described in Part One of this book) and are also sometimes unaware of the relationship between life events or strains and anxiety. These people will probably want the G.P. to give them something to help rid them of the anxiety signs immediately (particularly the physical ones) and the G.P. (because he or she may not have the time or training to look at the problem in more detail) responds by prescribing tranquillisers. These may well serve to 'deaden' the anxiety but, importantly, do not solve the problem which causes it, nor do they help the person learn more natural ways of dealing with stress and strain.

This book will help people learn techniques to help them cope with anxiety very effectively without the need for tranquillisers. However, if you are taking tranquillisers and wish to stop using them, it is important to do the following:

1 Arrange an appointment with your G.P. to discuss the best way of 'coming off' the tranquillisers. Suddenly stopping the tranquillisers can cause quite bad withdrawal effects for some people, so your G.P. will probably advise a gradual cutting down. You might find it useful to show the G.P. this book to help you explain to him or her what you are going to do yourself to help you learn to deal with the anxiety.

2 Make sure you have started putting into practice the techniques—particularly relaxation training—before you begin to cut down the tranquillisers.

3 Be prepared for some withdrawal effects for a few weeks (two to four) as you 'come off' the drug, as your body adjusts to doing without it. (If you have been on tranquillisers or sedatives for a long time you may find the withdrawal effects last longer.)

In the list of books and articles at the end of the book there are several publications mentioned which go into more detail about the problems associated with the use of tranquillisers, and you may find it useful to read these to give you further information. However, the most important point is that if you **learn** and then apply the approach described in this book, eventually you will be able to cope without the need of tranquillisers.

13 Summary

MAJOR POINTS OF PART ONE

1 Anxiety can be split into three different sides:
   (a) The physical side. This includes signs like palpitations, muscular tension, etc.
   (b) The psychological side. This has three areas:
      (i)   The **feelings** of fear
      (ii) The negative **thoughts/ideas** that worsen anxiety
      (iii) **Attitudes** and beliefs that can bring on and maintain anxiety.
   (c) The behavioural side. Including:
      (i) avoidance of various situations
      (ii) social behaviour which affects anxiety, particularly **passive/aggressive** compared to **assertive** styles of relating to people.

2 The physical signs and the feeling of fear are caused at higher levels by the switching on of the stress response. The stress response is a powerful, fast-acting, automatic mechanism which exists to help us deal with physical danger. It has developed over millions of years of evolution and its basic function is to make us highly aroused physically (leading to the various physical signs) and psychologically (leading to the feelings of emotionality, especially fear). Although we have evolved socially so that we face far less physical threat than our distant ancestors, our physical evolution has not yet caught up, so we still have this stress response, making the accidental triggering of anxiety signs highly likely. This is often experienced as panic attacks.

   At lower levels of anxiety, we enter the preparedness state which, like the stress response, is a natural and, at times, necessary mechanism we all have. The preparedness state enables us to become increasingly alert physically and mentally to help us deal more efficiently with (non-life-threatening) stresses, such as interviews. However, people can remain in the preparedness state when there is no external necessity. This will lead to feelings of being 'on edge' or nervous, as well as other signs such as sleeping problems, regular tension headaches, general tiredness, etc.

3 Stressful life events and life strains are often involved in bringing on and maintaining people's experience of anxiety. Life events are 'one off' occurrences, such as suffering a bereavement, being made redundant, being involved in an accident, etc. Life strains are **continuous** pressures, such as poverty, unemployment, relationship problems, etc.

Life events and life strains affect people (sometimes over a very long period of time) by:

(a) increasing people's overall level of tension (putting them in the preparedness state and making them increasingly vulnerable to further stresses)
(b) causing them to lose self-confidence/self-esteem, often without them being aware of this
(c) causing them to lose their sense of control, in other words creating a feeling of **helplessness**.

MAJOR POINTS OF PART TWO

1 (a) Relaxation training and physical exercise are powerful ways of reducing the physical signs of anxiety. Relaxation is a skill which works by reducing the **overall** level of physical arousal through concentrating on relieving **muscular** tension. At deeper states of relaxation feelings of mental calmness are also produced. Physical exercise can help the process of learning relaxation, as well as helping 'burn off' some of the physical side effects of high levels of tension.
(b) Approaches to dealing with the psychological side of anxiety involves:
  (i) changing specific thoughts which worsen anxiety, particularly thoughts which tend to be automatic

(ii) identifying attitudes and beliefs which are often long-standing and of which we are often unaware. Identifying the behaviours associated with these attitudes gives the key to changing them. Changing the behaviours which reflect attitudes is the best way of changing the attitudes themselves, although this will often be long-term in terms of the self-help programme.

(c) This self-help programme will involve:

(i) constructing hierarchies of situations which are currently avoided and gradually starting to work through these graded situations, so acquiring increasing confidence on the way

(ii) working out specific ways of behaving assertively in social situations, rather than passively or aggressively.

2 The first step in dealing with life events and life strains is to identify them. Some events and strains can be dealt with by employing the problem-solving technique to generate practical methods of approaching the difficulty. Some strains cannot be directly changed (for example unemployment) so ways of reducing their effects on the person are necessary. This is basically achieved by developing activities which will increase self-esteem and the sense of control.

3 These various approaches should be tailored to fit the needs of each individual. Different sides will be 'weighted' differently, depending on how much they are involved in the experience of anxiety.

4 Tranquillisers can be a source of difficulty for people, in that they may be found to be physically and psychologically addictive. The approaches outlined in this book will help people develop alternative methods of dealing with stress and anxiety, and for the person who wishes to learn to do without tranquillisers the best way is to use these methods and at the same time gradually reduce the use of tranquillisers, with the help of his or her G.P.

Appendix I   Progressive relaxation training

INTRODUCTION

The basic idea of relaxation training has been explained in Chapter 8. Before going on to the exercises themselves, we will go over a few points concerning how and when to practice relaxation, and then describe the importance of correct breathing:

1 Make relaxation exercises part of your normal daily routine. As we have seen, relaxation is a skill and so needs regular daily practice. Vary the times you do it initially until you find a time (or times) which suit you.

2 Don't worry if the relaxation exercises do not work for you initially. Keep persevering and you will soon be able to do it.

3 Make sure the room you use to do relaxation in is warm, comfortable and quiet. Make sure you are not disturbed; tell the family not to bother you, take the phone off the hook and so on.

4 The exercises involve tensing the various muscles, so take care when you are tensing them not to overdo it and strain the muscles. Concentrate most of your effort on the relaxation.

5 You can use relaxation in your day-to-day life by learning to recognise how tense you are in various situations, at work and at home, and then relaxing yourself. Even if you are just sitting watching T.V., be aware of tension creeping into various muscles, shoulder, neck and stomach muscles especially, and then relax those muscles.

6 People who experience higher than necessary tension levels tend also to be overactive, doing things more hurriedly and rushing about throughout the day. Learn to change this habit by slowing yourself down and taking things more easily (not easy if this has become a real habit, but remember all habits can be broken!).

7 Try to arrange to do the relaxation exercises after having done some physical exercise, as your muscles are then naturally prepared for relaxation.

8 Massage can be a very useful approach in dealing with tension, so it will probably be worthwhile arranging to have massage sessions from a qualified practitioner and/or by learning techniques from self-instructional books which you and a partner can then practice.

BREATHING EXERCISES

The technique of relaxation has two related parts:

1 Breathing exercises
2 Muscular relaxation

The two parts are incorporated in the following exercises but firstly you should bear in mind the importance of correct breathing as you do the exercises. When people become very anxious they invariably breathe rapidly. This rapid breathing serves to intensify various physical signs such as heart rate and dizziness. In fact, people often bring on anxiety attacks by starting to breathe very quickly. People may have told you to 'take deep breaths' to reduce the tension, but in fact this will worsen it if you take too many deep breaths. It is often helpful in anxiety-provoking situations to take one deep breath, then hold it for a few seconds, then slowly let the breath out, relaxing as you do so. Once you have done this aim at breathing slowly and gently. You may find this easier by concentrating on relaxing your stomach muscles as you breathe out. This is because if you are tense the powerful stomach muscles constrict the lower half of your lungs, and this leads to rapid 'shallow' breathing. So, as you breathe out, concentrate on relaxing, the stomach muscles in particular, and when you breathe in again, breathe air firstly into the bottom of the lungs (pushing your stomach outwards) and then into the rest of the lungs.

Finally, remember that correct breathing is a vitally important part of relaxation training, even though it may seem as though it is something which is so natural that it doesn't require attention. When you learn to be aware of the tension-worsening aspects of your breathing pattern, and replace it with a slow, regular, relaxation-inducing breathing pattern, you will have learned one of the keys to relaxation.

PROGRESSIVE MUSCLE RELAXATION TRAINING EXERCISES

RELAXATION OF ARMS (time 4–5 min)

Settle back as comfortably as you can. Let yourself relax to the best of your ability. . . Now, as you relax like that, clench your right fist, just clench your fist tighter and tighter, and study the tension as you do so. Keep it clenched and feel the tension in your right fist, hand, forearm. . .

And now relax. Let the fingers of your right hand become loose, and observe the contrast in your feelings. . . Now, let yourself go and try to become more relaxed all over. . . Once more, clench your right fist really tight. . . hold it, and notice the tension again. . .

Now let go, relax, let your fingers straighten out, and you notice the difference once more. . . Now repeat that with your left fist. Clench your left fist while the rest of your body relaxes, clench the fist tighter and feel the tension. . .

And now relax. Again enjoy the contrast. . . Repeat that once more, clench the left fist, tight and tense. . .

Now do the opposite of tension, relax and feel the difference. Continue relaxing like that for a while. . . Clench both fists tighter and tighter, both fists tense, forearms tense, study the sensations. . .

And relax. Straighten out your fingers and feel that relaxation. Continue relaxing your hands and forearms more and more. . . Now bend your elbows and tense your biceps, tense them harder and study the tension feelings. . .

Now, straighten out your arms, let them relax and feel the difference again. Let the relaxation develop. . . Once more, tense your biceps; hold the tension and observe it carefully. . .

Straighten the arms and relax; relax to the best of your ability. . . Each time, pay close attention to your feelings when you tense up and when you relax. Now straighten your arms and press your hands together so that you feel most tension in the triceps muscles along the back of your arms. Stretch your arms and press your hands together and feel the tension. . .

And now relax. Get your arms back into a comfortable position. Let the relaxation proceed on its own. The arms should feel comfortably heavy as you allow them to relax. . . Straighten the arms once more so that you feel the tension in the triceps muscles; straighten them. Feel that tension. . .

And relax. Now concentrate on pure relaxation in the arms without any tension. Get your arms comfortable and let them relax further and further. Continue relaxing your arms even further. Even when your arms seem fully relaxed, try to go that extra bit further; try to achieve deeper and deeper levels of relaxation.

RELAXATION OF FACIAL AREA WITH NECK, SHOULDERS AND UPPER BACK (time 4-5 min)

Let all your muscles go loose and heavy. Just settle back quietly and comfortably. Wrinkle up your forehead now; wrinkle it tighter. . .

And now stop wrinkling your forehead, relax and smooth it out. Picture the entire forehead and scalp becoming smoother as the relaxation increases. . . Now frown and crease your brows and study the tension. . .

Let go of the tension again. Smooth out the forehead once more. . . Now close your eyes tighter and tighter. . . Feel the tension. . .

And relax your eyes. Keep your eyes closed, gently, comfortably, and notice the relaxation. . . Now clench your jaws, bite your teeth together. Study the tension throughout the jaws. . .

Relax your jaws now. Let your lips part slightly. . . Appreciate the relaxation. . . Now press your tongue hard against the roof of your mouth. Look for tension. . .

Now let your tongue return to a comfortable and relaxed position. . . Now purse your lips, press your lips together tighter and tighter. . .

Relax the lips. Note the contrast between tension and relaxation. Feel the relaxation all over your face, all over your forehead and scalp, eyes, jaws, lips, tongue and throat. The relaxation progresses further and further. . .

Now attend to your neck muscles. Press your head back as far as it can go and feel the tension in the neck. Roll it to the right and feel the tension shift; now roll it to the left. Straighten your head and bring it forward, press your chin against your chest.

Let your head return to a comfortable position and study the relaxation. Let the relaxation develop. . . Shrug your shoulders, right up. Hold the tension. . .

Drop your shoulders and feel the relaxation. Neck and shoulders relaxed. . . Shrug your shoulders again and move them around. Bring your shoulders up and forward and back. Feel the tension in your shoulders and in your upper back.

Drop your shoulders once more and relax. Let the relaxation spread deep into the shoulders, right into your back muscles. Relax your neck and throat, and your jaws and other facial areas as the pure relaxation takes over and grows deeper. . . deeper. . . even deeper.

RELAXATION OF CHEST, STOMACH AND LOWER BACK (time 4–5 min)

Relax your entire body to the best of your ability. Feel the comfortable heaviness that accompanies relaxation. Breathe easily and freely in and out. Notice how the relaxation increases as you exhale. . . As you breathe out just feel that relaxation. . . Now breathe right in and fill your lungs. Inhale deeply and hold your breath. Study the tension. . .

Now exhale, let the walls of your chest grow loose and push the air out automatically. Continue relaxing and breathe freely and gently. Feel the relaxation and enjoy it. . . With the rest of your body as relaxed as possible, fill your lungs again. Breathe in deeply and hold it again. . .

Now, breathe out and appreciate the relief. Just breathe normally. Continue relaxing your chest and let the relaxation spread to your back, shoulders, neck and arms. Just let go. . . And enjoy the relaxation. Now pay attention to your abdominal muscles, your stomach area.

Tighten your stomach muscles, make your abdomen hard. Notice the tension. . .

And relax. Let the muscles loosen and notice the contrast. . . Once more, press and tighten your stomach muscles. Hold the tension and study it. . .

And relax. Notice the general well-being that comes with relaxing your stomach. . . Now draw your stomach in, pull the muscles right in and feel the tension this way. . .

Now relax again. Let your stomach out. Continue breathing normally and easily and feel the massaging action all over your chest and stomach. Now pull your stomach in again and hold the tension. . . Now push out and tense your muscles like that. Hold the tension. . . Once more pull in and feel the tension. . .

Now relax your stomach fully. Let the tension dissolve as the relaxation grows deeper. Each time you breathe out, notice the rhythmic relaxation both in your lungs and in your stomach. Notice how your chest and stomach relax more and more. . . Try to let go of all contractions anywhere in your body. . . Now direct your attention to your lower back. Arch up your back, make your lower back quite hollow, and feel the tension along your spine. . .

And settle down comfortably again relaxing the lower back. . . Just arch your back up and feel the tensions as you do so. Try to keep the rest of your body as relaxed as possible. Try to localise the tension throughout your lower back area. . .

Relax once more, relaxing further and further. Relax your lower back, relax your upper back, spread the relaxation to your stomach, chest, shoulders, arms and facial area. Relax these parts further and further and further and even deeper.

RELAXATION OF HIPS, THIGHS AND CALVES
FOLLOWED BY COMPLETE BODY RELAXATION

Let go of all tensions and relax. . . Now flex your buttocks and thighs. Flex your thighs by pressing down your heels as hard as you can. . .

Relax and note the difference. . . Straighten your knees and flex your thigh muscles again. Hold the tension. . .

Relax your hips and thighs. Allow the relaxation to proceed on its own. . . Press your feet and toes downwards, away from your face, so that your calf muscles become tense. Study that tension. . .

Relax your feet and calves. . . This time, bend your feet towards your face so that you feel tension along your shins. Bring your toes right up. . .

Relax again. Keep relaxing for a while. . . Now let yourself relax further all over. Relax your feet, ankles, calves and shins, knees, thighs, buttocks and hips. Feel the heaviness of your lower body as you relax still further. . . Now spread the relaxation to your stomach, waist, lower back. Let go more and more. Feel that relaxation all over. Let it proceed to your upper back, chest, shoulders and arms and right to the tips of your fingers. Keep relaxing more and more deeply. Make sure that no tension has crept into your throat; relax your neck and your jaws and all your facial muscles. Keep relaxing your whole body like that for a while. Let yourself relax.

Now you can deepen your level of relaxation by concentrating on breathing. Take one deep breath. . . Hold it for a few seconds. . . And then slowly let it out. Feel all the remaining tension draining away from your muscles as you do so. Carry on breathing slowly and gently. Each time you exhale relax all your muscles, the stomach muscles particularly. When you exhale, you don't need to use any muscles at all, so concentrate on letting go of tension as you breathe out.

Carry on relaxing like this for as long as you wish.

Appendix II Suggestions for further reading

The following list of books and articles is split into two parts. The first part gives a number of publications which either give more information about areas covered in this book, or give a different perspective on anxiety. Readers who have had or who are experiencing anxiety difficulties may find these publications particularly helpful.

The second part lists some publications which deal with the theory and research which has taken place recently concerning stress and anxiety. These publications will be especially useful to professionals (G.P.s, social workers, etc.) who would like to further their knowledge of some of the issues currently being discussed by workers in the field of stress and anxiety.

PART 1

Davis Smail, *Illusion and reality. The meaning of anxiety* (1984), J.M. Dent & Sons Ltd.

Luise Eichenbaum and Susie Orbach, *What do women want?* (1983), Fontana/Collins.

These two books have a psychotherapeutic approach to anxiety, the first book looking at anxiety from a philosophical basis, whilst the second is concerned with analysing psychological problems, including anxiety, as they are formed through experiences in early life. The second book is aimed particularly at women, but it is potentially very useful reading for men as well.

Trouble with tranquillisers (1982), Release Publications Ltd.

This short booklet gives some useful information about tranquillisers.

The XRB plan for physical fitness (1973), Penguin Books.

This inexpensive paperback gives a straightforward guide to developing a keep-fit programme.

Lucinda Lidell *et al.*, *The book of massage*, Ebury Press.

A straightforward guide to different techniques of massage.

PART 2

Barlow, D.H. & Wolfe, B.E. (1981). Behavioural approaches to anxiety disorders: a report on the NIMH-SUNY, Albany, Research Conference. *Journal of Consulting & Clinical Psychology*, **49**, No 3, 448-54.

Biran, M. & Wilson, G.T. (1981). Treatment of phobic disorders using cognitive and exposure methods: a self-efficacy analysis. *Journal of Consulting & Clinical Psychology*, 49, No. 6, 886-99.

Finlay-Jones, R. & Brown, G.W. (1981). Types of stressful life event and the onset of anxiety and depressive disorders. *Psychological Medicine*, 11, 803-15.

Hugdahl, K. (1981). The three-systems model of fear and emotion— a critical examination. *Behaviour Research and Therapy*, 19, 75-85.

Jacobsen, E. (1977). The origins and development of progressive relaxation. *Journal of Behaviour Therapy & Experimental Psychiatry*. 8, 119-23.

Meyer, V. & Reich, B. (1978). Anxiety management—the marriage of physiological and cognitive variables. *Behaviour Research & Therapy*, 16, 177-82.

Van Toller, C. (1979). *The nervous body: an introduction to the autonomic nervous system*. Wiley.